CATCH-UP
MATH
Get your child back on track!

T0267069

Whole Numbers ◉ Addition ◉ Subtraction

Multiplication ◉ Division ◉ Fractions

Decimals ◉ Measurement ◉ Area

Classifying Angles ◉ Time

Publishing Credits

Corinne Burton, M.A.Ed., *President* and *Publisher*
Emily R. Smith, M.A.Ed., *SVP of Content Development*
Véronique Bos, *VP of Creative*
Lynette Ordoñez, *Content Manager*
Avery Rabedeaux, *Assistant Editor*
Kevin Pham, *Graphic Designer*

Image Credits: all images from iStock, Dreamtime, and/or Shutterstock

Standards

© Copyright 2010 National Governors Association Center for Best Practices and Council of Chief State School Officers. All rights reserved.
© Copyright 2007–2023 Texas Education Agency (TEA). All Rights Reserved.
© 2023 TESOL International Association
© 2023 Board of Regents of the University of Wisconsin System

The classroom teacher may reproduce copies of materials in this book for classroom use only. The reproduction of any part for an entire school or school system is strictly prohibited. No part of this publication may be transmitted, stored, or recorded in any form without written permission from the publisher.

Website addresses included in this book are public domain and may be subject to changes or alterations of content after publication of this product. Shell Education does not take responsibility for the future accuracy or relevance and appropriateness of website addresses included in this book. Please contact the company if you come across any inappropriate or inaccurate website addresses, and they will be corrected in product reprints.

All companies, websites, and products mentioned in this book are registered trademarks of their respective owners or developers and are used in this book strictly for editorial purposes. No commercial claim to their use is made by the author(s) or the publisher.

A division of Teacher Created Materials

5482 Argosy Avenue
Huntington Beach, CA 92649
www.tcmpub.com/shell-education
ISBN 979-8-7659-7013-3
© 2024 Teacher Created Materials, Inc.

This Edition is for sale in North America (including Canada) only.
From material first published and copyright Pascal Press.

Printed by: **418**
Printed in: **USA**
PO#: **PO9308**

CONTENTS

CONTENTS

ABOUT CATCH-UP MATH

The Catch-Up Math series enables children to start from scratch when they are struggling with grade-level math. Each book takes math back to the foundation and ensures that all basic concepts are consolidated before moving forward. Lots of revision and opportunities to practice and build confidence are provided before moving on to new topics.

Each new topic is introduced clearly with simple explanations, examples and trial questions (with answers) before children move to the Practice section. To help students understand difficult topics, instructional videos are included throughout the book.

This book has 15 chapters that cover a variety of mathematical concepts. The chapters are:

SCAN to watch video

1 Whole Numbers

2 Addition

3 Subtraction

4 Multiplication

5 Division

6 Fractions

7 Decimals

8 Patterns

9 Length

10 Angles

11 Shapes

12 Area

13 Capacity

14 Mass

15 Time

A QR code on a topic page provides access to the video.

★ A review section that can be used as an assessment and to check children's progress is included at the end of each chapter.

★ Answers are at the back of the book.

How to use this book

Children can work through the pages from front to back or choose individual topics to reinforce areas where they are struggling.

The topics are introduced with:

- clear instructions, using simple language

- completed examples and incomplete examples for students to tackle before moving on to the **Your Turn** sections

- videos linked by QR codes to provide additional instruction and clarify difficult concepts

Each Your Turn section contains a SELF CHECK for students to reflect and give self-assessment on their understanding.

HOW TO USE THE QR CODES IN CATCH-UP MATH

A unique aspect of the **Catch-Up Math** series is the **instructional videos**.

The videos further explain and clarify various mathematical concepts. The videos are simply accessed via QR codes and can be watched on a phone or tablet. Or, view all the videos by following this link: tcmpub.digital/cu-math4.

Access the video by scanning the QR code with your device.

SCAN to watch video

Each video shows the page from the book. An instructor talks through the concepts and examples and demonstrates what students need to do. The solutions to the examples are presented before students tackle the **Your Turn** sections. This careful instruction ensures that children can confidently move on to the following Practice questions. Children should be encouraged to check their **Your Turn** answers before moving on.

25 instructional videos included!

WHOLE NUMBERS

ROUNDING TO 100 AND 1,000

Rounding is useful when you need to estimate an answer.

Round-down numbers	Round-up numbers
0 1 2 3 4	5 6 7 8 9

SCAN to watch video

Rounding to 100
1 Go to the hundreds column.
2 Write the round-up number above the hundreds.
3 Circle the number in the tens column.
4 Is it a round-up or round-down number?
5 Round your number.

Rounding to 1,000
1 Go to the thousands column.
2 Write the round-up number above the thousands.
3 Circle the number in the hundreds column.
4 Is it a round-up or round-down number?
5 Round your number.

If the number is less than 5, you round down. If the number is 5 or more, you round up.

Example 1:
Round 349 to the nearest 100.

4
349 ↙ down
300

Example 3:
Round 8,953 to the nearest 1,000. _____

Example 2:
Round 582 to the nearest 100.

6 ↖ up
582
600

Example 4:
Round 21,492 to the nearest 1,000. _____

Your turn

1 Round to the nearest 100.
a 653
_____
b 2,438
_____

2 Round to the nearest 1,000.
a 9,573
_____
b 24,252
_____

SELF CHECK   Mark how you feel
Got it!   Need help...   I don't get it

Check your answers
How many did you get correct?

© Shell Education

146435—Catch-Up Math   35

Scan this to access the video.

After watching the video, children can confidently complete the **Your Turn** section.

© Shell Education

MATH SKILLS

This book contains key math skills from both third and fourth grade to help your child catch up to grade level.

Grade 3 Math Skills	Pages
Understand place value, including the values of the digits in three- and four-digit numbers.	9–16, 21–26
Read and write numbers to 1,000 using numerals, words, and expanded form.	17–18
Round numbers to the nearest 10, 100, or 1,000.	35–36, 71–73
Add and subtract numbers under 1,000.	51–58, 61–68
Understand that multiplication problems represent groups multiplied by the number of objects in each group.	78–81
Apply properties of multiplication and division to multiply and divide numbers under 100.	82–87, 99–100
Understand that division problems represent a whole being divided into groups.	95–98
Understand that fractions are parts of wholes.	110–117
Use knowledge of numerators (number of parts) and denominators (the whole) to write fractions.	110–117
Compare fractions and identify equivalent fractions.	118–123
Find and explain patterns in a series of numbers.	138–141
Select and use appropriate tools to measure the lengths of objects.	146–150
Calculate the perimeter of a shape.	151–152, 188–189
Understand that shapes can be categorized based on their attributes (number of sides, number of parallel sides, etc.). Recognize rhombuses, rectangles, and squares as quadrilaterals.	166–169
Understand that area measures the space inside a shape and is measured in square units.	176–187
Find the area of a rectangle by multiplying its length by its width.	182–185
Measure and estimate liquid volumes and masses of objects using metric units and customary units.	196–203, 208–213
Solve word problems involving elapsed time.	219–222

Grade 4 Math Skills	Pages
Understand place value, including the values of the digits in four-digit numbers.	53–59
Read and write numbers to 1,000 using numerals, words, and expanded form.	49–50, 55–57
Round numbers to the nearest 10, 100, or 1,000.	47–48, 60–61
Find and explain patterns in a series of numbers.	27–28
Add and subtract numbers under 1,000.	78–79, 82–83, 97–98, 101–102
Understand that multiplication problems represent groups multiplied by the number of objects in each group.	106–107
Apply properties of multiplication and division to multiply and divide numbers under 100.	110–113
Understand that division problems represent a total number of objects divided into groups.	116–125
Understand that fractions are parts of wholes.	132–143
Use knowledge of numerators (number of parts) and denominators (the whole) to write fractions.	132–143
Compare fractions and identify equivalent fractions.	144–146
Create and interpret tables, picture graphs, and bar graphs with scaled intervals.	151–166
Use data in graphs and tables to solve "how many more" and "how many less" problems.	151–166
Understand that shapes can be categorized based on their attributes (number of sides, number of parallel sides, etc.). Recognize rhombuses, rectangles, and squares as quadrilaterals.	181–186
Understand that a square with a side length of 1 unit is called a unit square.	192–193
Find the area of a rectangle by multiplying its length by its width.	194–195
Measure and estimate liquid volumes and masses of objects using metric units and customary units.	199–206, 210–217
Solve word problems involving volumes or masses that are given in the same unit.	212–217

   © Shell Education

THREE-DIGIT NUMBERS

A three-digit number is a number that is made up of three numbers (or digits).

Numbers from 100 to 999 are three-digit numbers.

Here are some three-digit numbers: 236 529 106 240 911

Example 1:

The number 285 written in words is two hundred eighty-five.

The 2 has a value of 200.
The 8 has a value of 80.
The 5 has a value of 5.

Here is 285 in a chart:

Number	Hundreds	Tens	Ones
285	2	8	5

Example 2:

The number 946 written in words is _____ hundred _____-six.

The 9 has a value of _____.
The 4 has a value of _____.
The 6 has a value of _____.

Here is 946 in a chart:

Number	H	T	O
946	9		

Can you figure out how many three-digit numbers there are?

Your turn

Complete the chart.

	Number	Hundreds	Tens	Ones
	672	6	7	2
a	127			
b	249			
c	863			
d	524			
e	780			

SELF CHECK Mark how you feel

Got it! Need help... I don't get it

Check your answers
How many did you get correct?

PRACTICE

1 Write the following numbers in words.

- 657 six hundred fifty-seven
- a 293 ____________________
- b 451 ____________________
- c 764 ____________________
- d 503 ____________________
- e 850 ____________________
- f 300 ____________________

2 Complete the table.

	Number	Hundreds	Tens	Ones
●	259	2	5	9
a	410			
b	324			
c		5	6	8
d	879			
e		9	0	3

3 Circle with green all the numbers with 3 hundreds. Use blue for the numbers with 2 tens and red for the numbers with 8 ones.

(359)	319	218
721	838	422
347	748	362
924	109	300
432	685	426
188	923	878

© Shell Education

PLACE VALUE TO 1,000

The place value is the value of a digit based on
where it is in a number.

H T O

624

The place value of the 6
is hundreds because it is
in the hundreds place.

The place value of the 4
is ones because it is in
the ones place.

The place value of the 2 is tens
because it is in the tens place.

Example 1:
395 is a three-digit number that
has 3 hundreds, 9 tens, and 5 ones.

Look at the order of
the place value: first
hundreds, then tens,
and then ones.

hundreds
place

395

tens
place

ones
place

Example 2:
763 is a three-digit number that has

_____ hundreds, _____ tens, and _____ ones.

hundreds
place

763

tens
place

ones
place

**Your
turn**

1 What is the place value of the 8 in these numbers?

● 835 8 _____hundreds_____   c 781 8 _____

a 328 8 _____   d 498 8 _____

b 820 8 _____   e 482 8 _____

2 Circle the hundreds green, tens blue, and ones red.

       936   415   671   472   215

324   716   989   543   537

SELF CHECK   Mark how you feel

Got it!   Need help...   I don't get it

☺ ☐   😐 ☐   ☹ ☐

Check your answers

How many did
you get correct?

PRACTICE

 Write the numbers.

● 6 hundreds, 4 tens, 2 ones = __642__

a one ten, two hundreds, three ones = _____

b seven hundreds, five tens, eight ones = _____

c six tens, nine hundreds = _____

d five ones, five hundreds = _____

 **Circle the numbers with 5 tens.**

(257)	553	59	157	95
325	159	125	735	556
452	757	56	345	675

 Cross out the numbers with 9 hundreds.

937	795	195	94	987
93	909	993	496	890
98	982	957	973	921

What is the place value of the 7 in these numbers?

● 473   7 _____   **f** 497   7 _____

a 247   7 _____   **g** 715   7 _____

b 479   7 _____   **h** 17   7 _____

c 7   7 _____   **i** 79   7 _____

d 756   7 _____   **j** 647   7 _____

e 875   7 _____   **k** 709   7 _____

          © Shell Education

VALUE AND THREE-DIGIT NUMBERS

The value of a digit is how much it is worth.

Example 1:

724

The value of the 7 is 700.

The value of the 2 is 20.

The value of the 4 is 4.

Example 2:

136

The value of the 1 is _____.

The value of the 3 is _____.

The value of the 6 is _____.

Even though 1 is the smallest number, it has the greatest value as it is in the hundreds place.

Example 3:

859

The value of the 8 is _____.

The value of the 5 is _____.

The value of the 9 is _____.

Your turn

Circle in green the digit in each number with the most value and in red the digit with the least value.

⦿ ⑤9②   **e** 324   **j** 649

a 243   **f** 903   **k** 999

b 714   **g** 874   **l** 711

c 139   **h** 492   **m** 118

d 287   **i** 736   **n** 247

SELF CHECK   Mark how you feel

Got it!	Need help...	I don't get it
☐	☐	☐

Check your answers
How many did you get correct?

PRACTICE

 Write the numbers.

● 2 hundreds, 3 tens, 8 ones = __238__

a 3 hundreds, 7 tens, 1 one = _____

b 2 tens, 6 hundreds, 3 ones = _____

c 8 ones, 2 hundreds, 5 tens = _____

d 8 tens, 1 hundred, 4 ones = _____

e 9 hundreds, 9 ones, 8 tens = _____

 Circle the digits with a value of 6.

2⑥	326	246	624	6
643	62	861	16	746

 Circle the digits with a value of 70.

⑦8	27	872	79	777
7	127	737	175	474

 Circle the digits with a value of 800.

⑧32	849	28	8	863
847	189	888	782	148

5 **What is the value of the 4 in the following?**

● 439 __400__   **d** 342 _____   **h** 143 _____

a 48 _____   **e** 40 _____   **i** 470 _____

b 14 _____   **f** 47 _____   **j** 468 _____

c 436 _____   **g** 491 _____   **k** 4 _____

    © Shell Education

NUMBER EXPANDERS AND THREE-DIGIT NUMBERS

This number expander shows the number 273:

| 2 | hundreds | 7 | tens | 3 | ones |

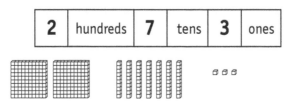

If we fold the number expander to make 273 using only tens and ones, we have:

| 2 | 7 | tens | 3 | ones |

If we fold the number expander again and make 273 using only ones, we have:

| 2 | 7 | 3 | ones |

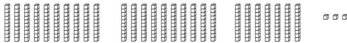

Look at the order of the place value: first hundreds, then tens, and then ones.

Your turn

Complete the number expanders.

● 872

| 8 | hundreds | 7 | tens | 2 | ones |

| 8 | 7 | tens | 2 | ones |

| 8 | 7 | 2 | ones |

a 184

| | hundreds | | tens | | ones |

| | tens | | ones |

| | ones |

SELF CHECK Mark how you feel

| Got it! | Need help... | I don't get it |

Check your answers
How many did you get correct?

1 Fill in the number expanders.

520

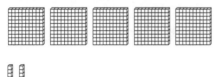

5	hundreds	2	tens	0	ones

		5	2	tens	0	ones

			5	2	0	ones

a 276

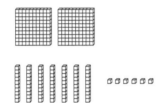

	hundreds		tens		ones

		tens		ones

			ones

b 605

	hundreds		tens		ones

		tens		ones

			ones

2 Write the number shown on each number expander.

7	2	5	ones

_725_

b

5	hundreds	0	tens	4	ones

_____

a

3	2	tens	6	ones

_____

c

9	0	6	ones

_____

3 Fill in the number expanders.

423

4	2	3	ones

b 724

	hundreds		tens		ones

a 342

		tens		ones

c 649

			ones

EXPANDED THREE-DIGIT NUMBERS

Expanding a number is writing the number
to show the value of each digit.

Example 1: 27 =   20   +   7
                (2 tens)   (7 ones)

Example 2: 53 =   50   +   3
                (5 tens)   (3 ones)

Example 3: 198 =   100   +   90 + 8
          (____ hundreds) (____ tens) (____ ones)

Example 4: 346 =   ____   +   ____ + ____
          (____ hundreds) (____ tens) (____ ones)

Numbers written like this
are in "expanded form."

Your
turn

Expand the numbers.

● 734 = _700_ + _30_ + _4_

    = _7_ hundreds + _3_ tens + _4_ ones

a 265 = ____ + ____ + ____

    = ____ hundreds + ____ tens + ____ ones

b 638 = ____ + ____ + ____

    = ____ hundreds + ____ tens + ____ ones

SELF CHECK   Mark how you feel

Got it!	Need help...	I don't get it
☐	☐	☐

Check your answers
How many did
you get correct?

PRACTICE

Match each number to its expanded form.

- ● 394   800 + 50

- **a** 727   600 + 7

- **b** 850   500 + 80 + 2

- **c** 607   300 + 90 + 4

- **d** 582   400 + 90 + 5

- **e** 500   700 + 20 + 7

- **f** 495   500

2 Write these numbers in expanded form.

- ● 923 __900 + 20 + 3__   **d** 206 _____

- **a** 410 _____   **e** 300 _____

- **b** 359 _____   **f** 783 _____

- **c** 832 _____   **g** 564 _____

3 Complete.

- ● 600 + 40 + 1 = __641__   **g** 100 + 40 + 3 = _____

- **a** 100 + 90 = _____   **h** 900 + 80 + 4 = _____

- **b** 400 + 30 = _____   **i** 400 + 80 + 7 = _____

- **c** 700 + 40 + 1 = _____   **j** 300 + 70 + 6 = _____

- **d** 200 + 50 + 2 = _____   **k** 600 + 10 + 2 = _____

- **e** 300 + 50 + 5 = _____   **l** 500 + 30 + 8 = _____

- **f** 800 + 2 = _____

© Shell Education

FOUR-DIGIT NUMBERS

A four-digit number is a number that is made up of four numbers (or digits).

Numbers from 1,000 to 9,999 are four-digit numbers.

Here are some four-digit numbers:

4,873   2,972   5,097   6,203   4,200

Example 1: 3,946

The number 3,946 has four digits. Written in words, it is three thousand nine hundred forty-six.

The 3 has a value of 3,000.
The 9 has a value of 900.
The 4 has a value of 40.
The 6 has a value of 6.

Here is 3,946 in a chart:

Number	Th	H	T	O
3,946	3	9	4	6

Example 2: 2,873
The number 2,873 in words is

_____

_____

_____

In a number chart it is:

Number	Th	H	T	O
2,873				

Your turn

Complete the chart.

	Number	Th	H	T	O	Words
●	2,319	2	3	1	9	two thousand three hundred nineteen
a	4,692					four thousand six hundred ninety-two
b	5,300					

SELF CHECK   Mark how you feel
Got it!   Need help...   I don't get it

Check your answers
How many did you get correct?

PRACTICE

1 Write these numbers in words.

⬤ 2,495 __two thousand four hundred ninety-five__

a 7,219 _____

b 3,490 _____

c 2,005 _____

d 8,943 _____

2 Put these numbers in ascending order. Write a 1 in the box under the smallest number, 2 in the box under the next largest number, and so on.

⬤ 1,429 1,325 1,703 1,421
  [3]   [1]   [4]   [2]

b 7,375 4,283 6,154 1,095
  [ ]   [ ]   [ ]   [ ]

a 2,150 5,125 1,253 1,520
  [ ]   [ ]   [ ]   [ ]

c 2,493 3,286 1,078 2,197
  [ ]   [ ]   [ ]   [ ]

3 Order these numbers in descending order by putting a 1 in the box under the largest number and a 4 in the box under the smallest number.

⬤ 8,621 9,235 4,396 6,981
  [2]   [1]   [4]   [3]

b 6,123 9,583 1,252 9,525
  [ ]   [ ]   [ ]   [ ]

a 1,325 5,937 9,377 9,529
  [ ]   [ ]   [ ]   [ ]

c 6,303 9,524 3,781 8,874
  [ ]   [ ]   [ ]   [ ]

4 Write these words in numbers.

⬤ three thousand two hundred sixteen __3,216__

a four thousand nine hundred twenty-two _____

b eight thousand three _____

c seven thousand four hundred sixty-nine _____

    © Shell Education

PLACE VALUE AND FOUR-DIGIT NUMBERS

The place value is the value of a digit based on where it is in a number.

Th H T O

The place value of the 3 is thousands because it is in the thousands place.

The place value of the 8 is ones because it is in the ones place.

The place value of the 5 is hundreds because it is in the hundreds place.

The place value of the 2 is tens because it is in the tens place.

Example 1: 3,528 has 3 thousands, 5 hundreds, 2 tens, and 8 ones.

Th	H	T	O
3	5	2	8

thousands — 3,528 — ones
hundreds   tens

Example 2:

4,930 has ____ thousands, ____ hundreds, ____ tens, and ____ ones.

Th	H	T	O
4			0

thousands — 4,930 — ones
hundreds tens

Example 3:

8,972 has ____ thousands, ____ hundreds, ____ tens, and ____ ones.

Th	H	T	O
8		7	

Your turn

Circle the thousands purple, the hundreds green, the tens blue, and the ones red.

3,921   4,374   5,500   9,746   9,525

2,125   5,251   6,303   1,609

SELF CHECK Mark how you feel

Got it! □   Need help... □   I don't get it □

Check your answers
How many did you get correct?

PRACTICE

 Write the numbers.

⬤ 6 thousands, 3 hundreds, 4 tens, 5 ones = <u>6,345</u>

a 8 hundreds, 1 thousand, 8 tens, 2 ones = _____

b 7 ones, 4 tens, 3 thousands = _____

c 6 thousands, 3 tens = _____

d 8 tens, 2 hundreds, 9 thousands = _____

 Complete the chart.

	Number	Thousands	Hundreds	Tens	Ones
⬤	2,491	2	4	9	1
a	3,269				
b	9,038				
c		4	7	3	0
d		5	4	7	6
e		6	9	2	4

3 Circle the following numbers in
red for the numbers with 6 ones
blue for the numbers with 8 tens
green for the numbers with 1 hundred
purple for the numbers with 4 thousands.

(4,372)   4,362   6,153   1,956   6,666

1,483   2,140   8,147   3,482   4,040

3,206   2,736   3,884   4,711   1,134   3,381

4,370   5,296   8,706   9,283   4,635

1,782   8,132   4,975   4,125   3,776

© Shell Education

VALUE AND FOUR-DIGIT NUMBERS

The value of a number is how much it is worth.

Th H T O

The value of the 8 is 8,000. ➡ **8,632** ⬅ The value of the 2 is 2.

The value of the 6 is 600.   The value of the 3 is 30.

Example 1: 1,745

In 1,745, even though 1 is the smallest number, it has the greatest value because it is in the thousands place.
The 1 is worth the most. It is worth 1,000.
The 7 is worth 700, the 4 is worth 40, and the 5 is worth 5.

Example 2: 3,472

The 3 is worth the most. It is worth _____.

The 4 is worth ____, the 7 is worth ____, and

the 2 is worth ____.

Example 3: 1,397

The ____ is worth the most. It is worth _____.

The 3 is worth ____, the 9 is worth ____, and

the ____ is worth ____ .

When you put a number in a different place, it has a different value.

![star] **Your turn**

1 Circle the numbers where the value of the 8 is 8,000.

8,432   847   18   836   82

78   81   8,936

2 For each number, use red to circle the digit worth the most and blue to circle the digit worth the least.

Ⓐ,29④   1,157   458   3,866   5,490

8,745   8,894   6,128

SELF CHECK   Mark how you feel
Got it!   Need help...   I don't get it

Check your answers
How many did you get correct?

PRACTICE

 1 Circle the numbers where the value of the 4 is 40.

(248)   24   463   74   142

640   4,925   458   4,710   343

2 Circle the numbers where the value of 5 is 500.

(536)   53   25   524   5,382

5,920   599   56   507   5

3 What is the value of the 4 in these numbers?

● 842   _40_

a 429 _____   f 849 _____   l 4 _____

b 94 _____   g 74 _____   m 4,306 _____

c 347 _____   h 463 _____   n 2,934 _____

d 4,913 _____   i 4,739 _____   o 8,740 _____

e 14 _____   j 5,241 _____   p 3,497 _____

k 9,437 _____   q 4,978 _____

4 What is the value of the underlined digit?

● 6<u>3</u>8   _30_

a 49<u>1</u> _____   f 1,1<u>2</u>5 _____   l 2<u>4</u>5 _____

b 1,<u>3</u>57 _____   g <u>2</u>,543 _____   m <u>8</u>,095 _____

c <u>9</u>,300 _____   h 3,93<u>0</u> _____   n 6<u>7</u> _____

d 6,1<u>3</u>1 _____   i 1,<u>6</u>31 _____   o <u>7</u>61 _____

e 62<u>3</u> _____   j <u>3</u>,421 _____   p 3<u>5</u> _____

k 5,<u>9</u>30 _____   q 12<u>6</u> _____

   © Shell Education

NUMBER EXPANDERS AND FOUR-DIGIT NUMBERS

The number expander shows 1,324.

Example 1:

1	thousand	3	hundreds	2	tens	4	ones

= × 1   × 3   × 2   × 4

We can make the same number using hundreds, tens, and ones.

1	3	hundreds	2	tens	4	ones

= × 13   × 2   × 4

Here 1,324 is made using only tens, and ones.

1	3	2	tens	4	ones

= × 132   × 4

Now 1,324 is made only using ones.

1	3	2	4	ones

= × 1,324

Example 2: Complete the number expanders for 6,845.

6	Th	8	H	4	T	5	0

		6	8	H	4	T		0

					T	5	0

	6				0

Your turn

Fill in the gaps.

6	8	4	3
	68	4	3
		684	3
			6843

a

7	4	0	6

SELF CHECK   Mark how you feel

Got it!   Need help...   I don't get it

Check your answers
How many did you get correct?

PRACTICE

  Match the blocks with the number expanders.

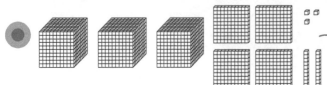

2	Th	2	H	5	T	1	0

a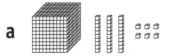

3	Th	5	H	4	T	5	0

b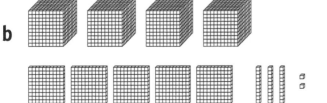

3	Th	4	H	2	T	3	0

c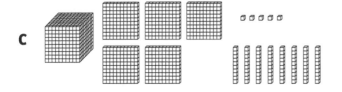

4	Th	5	H	3	T	2	0

d

1	Th	5	H	8	T	5	0

e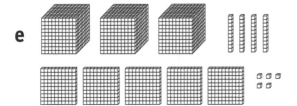

1	Th	0	H	3	T	6	0

  Write each number shown on the number expander.

4	7	2	tens	9	ones

4,729

b
2	Th	4	H	6	T	8	0

_____

a
8	5	3	2	ones

_____

c
7	5	H	6	T	4	0

_____

© Shell Education

EXPANDED FOUR-DIGIT NUMBERS

You can show numbers using Base 10 blocks, an abacus, and expanded form.

Example 1:

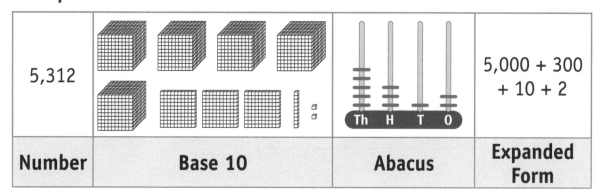

Number	Base 10	Abacus	Expanded Form
5,312			5,000 + 300 + 10 + 2

Example 2:

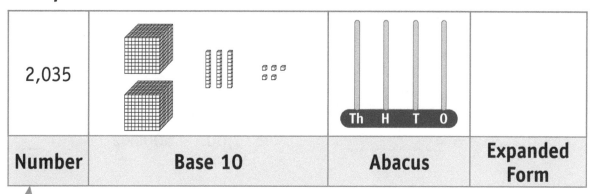

Number	Base 10	Abacus	Expanded Form
2,035			

Your turn

Complete the table.

Number	Base 10	Abacus	Expanded Form
1,126			
2,315			

SELF CHECK Mark how you feel

Got it!	Need help...	I don't get it
☐	☐	☐

Check your answers
How many did you get correct?

© Shell Education

PRACTICE

 1 Write these four-digit numbers in expanded form.

⬤ 1,832 = __1,000 + 800 + 30 + 2__

a 3,627 = _____

b 4,803 = _____

c 5,093 = _____

d 2,222 = _____

e 7,640 = _____

 2 Write these numbers in expanded form.

⬤ 5,000 + 200 + 50 + 3 = _5,253_   **c** 9,000 + 900 = _____

a 6,000 + 300 + 10 + 2 = _____   **d** 4,000 + 200 + 3 = _____

b 7,000 + 20 + 5 = _____   **e** 1,000 + 500 + 20 + 7 = _____

 3 Complete the table.

Number	Base 10	Abacus	Expanded Form
1,223		Th H T O	1,000 + 200 + 20 + 3
2,339		Th H T O	
3,459		Th H T O	

© Shell Education

ORDERING FOUR-DIGIT NUMBERS

Ascending order is when numbers are ordered from smallest to largest. These numbers are in ascending order: 3,256, 4,815, 7,394, 8,216, 9,018.

Descending order is when numbers are ordered from largest to smallest. Now the numbers are rearranged into descending order: 9,018, 8,216, 7,394, 4,815, 3,256.

Remember – "descending" has a d for down; the numbers are going down.

Example 1:

Write these numbers in ascending order.
6,258, 3,724, 9,215, 4,711, 9,283

| 3,724 | 4,711 | 6,258 | 9,215 | 9,283 |

Example 2:

Write these numbers in descending order.
6,258, 3,724, 9,215, 4,711, 9,283

| | | | | |

Your turn

1 Order these numbers in ascending order.

● 2,473, 1,215, 3,791, 3,971 1,215 2,473 3,791 3,971

a 5,253, 9,691, 8,873, 3,788 _____

b 6,740, 2,440, 9,894, 6,440 _____

2 Order these numbers in descending order.

a 2,020, 1,936, 7,791, 3,719 _____

b 2,904, 1,973, 1,503, 7,179 _____

SELF CHECK Mark how you feel

Got it!	Need help...	I don't get it
☺ ☐	😐 ☐	☹ ☐

Check your answers
How many did you get correct?

PRACTICE

 1 Label the numbers in ascending order from 1 (smallest) to 5 (largest).

● 5,217   3,284   7,190   6,177   2,849
   [3]   [2]   [5]   [4]   [1]

a 9,037   9,730   9,073   9,307   9,703
      □   □   □   □   □

b 7,213   3,127   2,137   1,723   1,327
      □   □   □   □   □

c 9,876   6,879   8,967   7,896   6,987
      □   □   □   □   □

d 2,496   6,942   6,429   6,400   6,404
      □   □   □   □   □

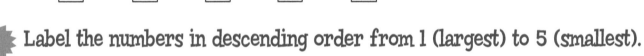

2 Label the numbers in descending order from 1 (largest) to 5 (smallest).

● 2,606   3,295   1,273   4,915   5,231
   [4]   [3]   [5]   [2]   [1]

a 7,312   2,137   7,321   7,123   7,231
      □   □   □   □   □

b 5,243   7,819   5,013   3,310   2,440
      □   □   □   □   □

c 7,217   9,524   1,806   2,449   9,373
      □   □   □   □   □

d 8,532   2,964   1,425   5,400   4,500
      □   □   □   □   □

© Shell Education

GREATER THAN, EQUAL TO, LESS THAN

>	=	<
the symbol for greater than	the symbol for equal to	the symbol for less than

Example 1: 453 | > | 249

Read from left to right:

Is 453 greater than (>) 249?   ✓ Yes

Is 453 equal to (=) 249?   ✗ No

Is 453 less than (<) 249?   ✗ No

> Which number does the pointy end point to? That helps you tell the difference between < and >.

Example 2: 1,275 | = | 1,275

Is 1,275 greater than (>) 1,275?   ✗ No

Is 1,275 equal to (=) 1,275?   ✓ Yes

Is 1,275 less than (<) 1,275?   ✗ No

Example 3: 2,410 ☐ 6,870

Is 2,410 greater than (>) 6,870?   _____

Is 2,410 equal to (=) 6,870?   _____

Is 2,410 less than (<) 6,870?   _____

Your turn

Write True or False.

● 1,010 < 2,734   _True_   **c** 434 > 109   _____

a 7,145 > 6,243   _____   **d** 6,251 < 1,290   _____

b 1,315 = 1,315   _____   **e** 745 > 893   _____

SELF CHECK	Mark how you feel	
Got it!	Need help...	I don't get it
😊 ☐	😐 ☐	😟 ☐

Check your answers
How many did you get correct?

PRACTICE

 Fill in the missing symbols.

● 473 $\boxed{<}$ 792   **c** 103 $\boxed{\phantom{<}}$ 103   **f** 545 $\boxed{\phantom{<}}$ 711

a 129 $\boxed{\phantom{<}}$ 792   **d** 461 $\boxed{\phantom{<}}$ 416   **g** 813 $\boxed{\phantom{<}}$ 318

b 925 $\boxed{\phantom{<}}$ 127   **e** 382 $\boxed{\phantom{<}}$ 283   **h** 207 $\boxed{\phantom{<}}$ 720

 Write the words $\boxed{\text{is greater than}}$, $\boxed{\text{is equal to}}$, or $\boxed{\text{is less than}}$ **to make these true.**

● 173 | is less than | 472   **e** 523 | | 523

a 321 | | 123   **f** 920 | | 902

b 841 | | 426   **g** 747 | | 774

c 909 | | 836   **h** 209 | | 209

d 417 | | 714   **i** 345 | | 304

 Circle the numbers that match the descriptions.

● **more than 73**   (102) (78) 58 73 (89) (95) 70

a **less than 21**   21 73 29 19 16 42 37 18

b **more than 93**   93 47 94 16 95 39 98

c **less than 87**   87 89 73 17 41 82 9

d **more than 325**   129 325 392 145 463 173 497

e **equal to 127**   127 721 127 127 371 271 128

f **less than 432**   432 317 324 147 214 234 541

g **equal to 607**   607 706 176 607 607 67 167

   © Shell Education

4 Fill in the missing symbols.

    • 2,417 $\boxed{<}$ 7,412   **d** 3,857 $\boxed{\phantom{<}}$ 7,583   **h** 5,678 $\boxed{\phantom{<}}$ 8,765

    a 7,600 $\boxed{\phantom{<}}$ 7,006   **e** 2,934 $\boxed{\phantom{<}}$ 4,932   **i** 9,930 $\boxed{\phantom{<}}$ 9,033

    b 2,491 $\boxed{\phantom{<}}$ 2,491   **f** 5,921 $\boxed{\phantom{<}}$ 5,912   **j** 2,011 $\boxed{\phantom{<}}$ 2,020

    c 8,491 $\boxed{\phantom{<}}$ 1,459   **g** 6,030 $\boxed{\phantom{<}}$ 6,300   **k** 6,292 $\boxed{\phantom{<}}$ 6,922

5 Write three numbers greater than the number shown.

    • 4,352   _4,532_   _4,590_   _6,511_

    a 5,231   _____   _____   _____

    b 6,593   _____   _____   _____

    c 5,847   _____   _____   _____

    d 9,458   _____   _____   _____

6 Write three numbers less than the number shown.

    • 5,249   _5,010_   _4,132_   _1,754_

    a 7,342   _____   _____   _____

    b 8,294   _____   _____   _____

    c 9,311   _____   _____   _____

    d 6,425   _____   _____   _____

7 Write a number in between.

    • 1,247 $\boxed{1,389}$ 1,435   **c** 2,854 $\boxed{}$ 5,859

    a 3,136 $\boxed{}$ 4,425   **d** 935 $\boxed{}$ 1,034

    b 2,634 $\boxed{}$ 2,723   **e** 3,649 $\boxed{}$ 3,784

8 Write True or False.

⬤ 2,432 < 6,295 ___True___   e 5,740 = 5,704 _____

a 7,143 > 2,163 _____   f 9,386 > 1,057 _____

b 2,409 = 2,409 _____   g 6,322 < 6,895 _____

c 5,382 < 5,163 _____   h 9,855 < 9,981 _____

d 8,740 = 8,740 _____   i 7,249 < 7,942 _____

 9 Circle the numbers that match the descriptions.

⬤ **more than 125**   (192) 125 (127) 124 (291) (129)

a **less than 626**   620   662   262   668   266   594   694

b **equal to 714**   714   741   417   174   714   471   147   714

c **less than 422**   422   224   442   424   142   242   422

d **equal to 928**   299   928   829   928   298   928

e **more than 1,253** 5,231 1,352 1,253 1,235 1,325 1,523 1,253

f **more than 9,727** 9,727 9,729 7,729 9,772 9,727 7,927 2,779

g **less than 3,493** 3,493 3,439 4,393 3,394 9,433 3,499 3,493

h **equal to 8,352**   5,382 2,583 8,352 8,352 3,852 2,835 8,352

10 Circle the correct symbol

⬤ 343 | ⟩ = < | 249   e 425 | > = < | 462

a 648 | > = < | 846   f 860 | > = < | 796

b 728 | > = < | 320   g 947 | > = < | 780

c 103 | > = < | 103   h 581 | > = < | 343

d 242 | > = < | 585   i 669 | > = < | 468

© Shell Education

ROUNDING TO 100 AND 1,000

Rounding is useful when you need to estimate an answer.

SCAN to watch video

Round-down numbers	Round-up numbers
← 0 1 2 3 4	5 6 7 8 9 →

Rounding to 100

1 Go to the hundreds column.
2 Write the round-up number above the hundreds.
3 Circle the number in the tens column.
4 Is it a round-up or round-down number?
5 Round your number.

Rounding to 1,000

1 Go to the thousands column.
2 Write the round-up number above the thousands.
3 Circle the number in the hundreds column.
4 Is it a round-up or round-down number?
5 Round your number.

If the number is less than 5, you round down. If the number is 5 or more, you round up.

Example 1:
Round 349 to the nearest 100.

4
3(4)9 ↶ down
300

Example 2:
Round 582 to the nearest 100.

6 ↶ up
5(8)2
600

Example 3:
Round 8,953 to the nearest 1,000.

_____
_____

Example 4:
Round 21,492 to the nearest 1,000.

_____
_____

Your turn

1 Round to the nearest 100.

a 653

_____

b 2,438

_____

2 Round to the nearest 1,000.

a 9,573

_____

b 24,252

_____

SELF CHECK   Mark how you feel
Got it! □   Need help... □   I don't get it □

Check your answers
How many did you get correct?

© Shell Education

PRACTICE

 1 Round these numbers to the nearest 100.

      6
● 3,5②4   **c** 963   **f** 1,590
  3,500 ___   _____   _____

a 1,725   **d** 1,043   **g** 4,923

_____   _____   _____

b 257   **e** 2,597   **h** 648

_____   _____   _____

 2 Round these numbers to the nearest 1,000.

      8
● 7,②95   **b** 4,935   **d** 6,259

_____   _____   _____

a 3,428   **c** 7,135   **e** 2,843

_____   _____   _____

 3 Round these numbers to the nearest 100, then 1,000.

● 2,593   **c** 8,395

  nearest 100   2,600   nearest 100 _____
  nearest 1,000 3,000   nearest 1,000 _____

a 4,938   **d** 4,723

  nearest 100 _____   nearest 100 _____
  nearest 1,000 _____   nearest 1,000 _____

b 3,142   **e** 6,492

  nearest 100 _____   nearest 100 _____
  nearest 1,000 _____   nearest 1,000 _____

         © Shell Education

FIVE-DIGIT NUMBERS

A five-digit number is made up of five numbers (or digits).
Numbers in the ten thousands have five digits:
10,000 to 99,999.

Here are some five-digit numbers:

39,256   73,824   19,003   24,893

Example 1:

23,495 is written as twenty-three thousand
four hundred ninety-five.

Read the
numbers aloud
to help you
work out how
to write them.

Example 2:

19,053 is written as nineteen thousand fifty-three.

Example 3: 60,425 is written as sixty _____
four _____ _____-_____.

Example 4: 42,950 is written as forty-_____ thousand
_____ hundred _____.

Your turn

1 Circle the five-digit numbers.

(24,957)   1,003   42,056   73,950   26,435
7,632   7,458   17,537   835

2 Match the numbers to the words.

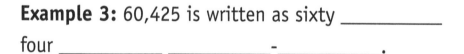

● 28,419   seventy-three thousand four hundred twenty

a 73,420   twenty-eight thousand four hundred nineteen

b 19,596   nineteen thousand five hundred ninety-six

c 84,253   eighty-four thousand two hundred fifty-three

SELF CHECK   Mark how you feel

Got it!	Need help...	I don't get it

Check your answers
How many did
you get correct?

PRACTICE

 Write these numbers in words.

⬤ 23,976 <u>twenty-three thousand nine hundred seventy-six</u>

a 49,350

_____

b 57,420

_____

c 62,943

_____

d 81,462

_____

e 93,258

_____

f 16,422

_____

 Match these numbers to the words.

⬤ 47,215 ⎯⎯⎯⎯⎯⎯   ninety-four thousand three hundred eighty-two

a 53,847 ⎯⎯⎯⎯⎯   forty-seven thousand two hundred fifteen

b 71,329   sixty-two thousand four hundred seventy-one

c 94,382   seventy-six thousand two hundred eighteen

d 81,432   seventy-one thousand three hundred twenty-nine

e 76,218   thirty-one thousand two hundred forty

f 62,471   fifty-three thousand eight hundred forty-seven

g 31,240   eighty-one thousand four hundred thirty-two

© Shell Education

PLACE VALUE TO 100,000

The place value is the value of a digit based on where it is in a number.

37,289 is a five-digit number.

TT Th H T O

37,289

The place value of the 3 is ten thousands because it is in the ten thousands place.

The place value of the 7 is thousands because it is in the thousands place.

The place value of the 2 is hundreds because it is in the hundreds place.

The place value of the 9 is ones because it is in the ones place.

The place value of the 8 is tens because it is in the tens place.

Example 1:

37,289 has 3 ten thousands, 7 thousands, 2 hundreds, 8 tens, and 9 ones.

ten thousands — 3 7, 2 8 9 — ones
thousands hundreds tens

This is 37,289 in a place value chart:

TT	Th	H	T	O
3	7	2	8	9

Example 2: 47,568 has _____ ten thousands, _____ thousands,

5 _____, 6 tens, and 8 _____.

This is 47,568 in a place value chart:

TT	Th	H	T	O

Look at the spacing between the thousands place and the hundreds place.

Your turn

Circle the ten thousands orange, the thousands purple, the hundreds green, the tens blue, and the ones red.

73,608   89,243   63,825   74,103

61,000   47,090   32,361   24,140

SELF CHECK   Mark how you feel

Got it!	Need help...	I don't get it

Check your answers

How many did you get correct?

PRACTICE

1 Write these numbers.

⬤ 27 thousands, 6 tens, 2 hundreds ___27,260___

a 2 ten thousands, 3 tens, 4 hundreds, 1 ones _____

b 94 thousands, 6 ones, 7 hundreds, 3 tens _____

c 5 tens, 6 hundreds, 5 ones, 35 thousands _____

d 6 ten thousands, 8 ones, 2 hundreds, 5 thousands, 1 tens _____

2 Complete the chart.

	Number	Ten thousands	Thousands	Hundreds	Tens	Ones
⬤	34,398	3	4	3	9	8
a	67,138					
b	15,840					
c		7	1	4	5	9
d		2	5	0	4	3
e	75,458					

3 Write the numbers in the correct place on the chart.

		Ten thousands	Thousands	Hundreds	Tens	Ones
⬤	60,000	60,000				
a	5,000					
b	2					
c	10					
d	80,000					
e	5					
f	80					

   © Shell Education

THE VALUE OF NUMBERS TO 100,000

The value of a number is how much it is worth.

Example 1:

H T O

The value of the 6 is 600. ➡ **692** ⬅ The value of the 2 is 2.

⬆

The value of the 9 is 90.

Example 2:

Th H T O

The value of the 3 is 3,000. ➡ **3,685** ⬅ The value of the 5 is 5.

The value of the 6 is 600. ⬆⬆ The value of the 8 is 80.

Example 3:

TT Th H T O

The value of the 2 is _____. ➡ **24,769** ⬅ The value of the 9 is _____.

The value of the 4 is _____. ⬆⬆⬆ The value of the 6 is _____.

The value of the 7 is _____.

Your turn

Circle in green the digit with the most value and in red the digit with the least value.

● ②8,49①   10,398   24,937   82,358

90,009   12,683   73,469   44,444

35,293   47,247   64,293

SELF CHECK   Mark how you feel

Got it!	Need help...	I don't get it
☺ ☐	😐 ☐	☹ ☐

Check your answers
How many did you get correct?

PRACTICE

1 Write numbers using these digits:

3 5 8 7 6

● 6 hundreds ___3,687___   e 5 ten thousands _____

a 3 ten thousands _____   f 3 tens _____

b 8 hundreds _____   g 5 ones _____

c 7 thousands _____   h 7 hundreds _____

d 6 ones _____   i 7 ten thousands _____

2 Write the missing numbers to make 32,487.

● 32 thousands + ___487___   c 32,487 ones + _____

a 3 ten thousands + _____   d 3,248 tens + _____

b 324 hundreds + _____

3 What is the value of the underlined digit?

● 24,7̲31 = ___700___   j 41,27̲3 = _____

a 3̲8,420 = _____   k 81,̲431 = _____

b 16,21̲6 = _____   l 57,6̲31 = _____

c 4̲1,249 = _____   m 24,62̲2 = _____

d 72,̲542 = _____   n 8̲1,030 = _____

e 31,0̲53 = _____   o 60̲,239 = _____

f 17,45̲8 = _____   p 4̲8,346 = _____

g 9̲1,004 = _____   q 34,̲189 = _____

h 85,37̲2 = _____   r 97,25̲7 = _____

i 21,4̲35 = _____   s 67̲,201 = _____

© Shell Education

GREATER THAN, EQUAL TO, LESS THAN: NUMBERS TO 100,000

| **>** greater than | **=** equal to | **<** less than |

SCAN to watch video

Example 1: 13,157 $\boxed{<}$ 23,546

Read from left to right. Ask yourself:

Is 13,157 greater than (>) 23,546?   ✗ No

Is 13,157 equal to (=) 23,546?   ✗ No

Is 13,157 less than (<) 23,546?   ✓ Yes

Example 2: 34,957 $\boxed{=}$ 34,957

Is 34,957 greater than (>) 34,957?   ✗ No

Is 34,957 equal to (=) 34,957?   ✓ Yes

Is 34,957 less than (<) 34,957?   ✗ No

> Which number does the pointy end point to? That helps you tell the difference between < and >.

Example 3: 49,520 $\boxed{}$ 15,490

Is 49,520 greater than (>) 15,490?   _____

Is 49,520 equal to (=) 15,490?   _____

Is 49,520 less than (<) 15,490?   _____

Your turn

Answer Yes or No.

⦿ Is 65,249 < 57,957?   <u>No</u>

a Is 14,573 > 24,297?   _____

b Is 36,429 < 59,419?   _____

c Is 41,000 = 41,000?   _____

SELF CHECK   **Mark how you feel**

| Got it! | Need help... | I don't get it |

Check your answers
How many did you get correct?

PRACTICE

1 Insert the correct symbol: >, <, or =.

24,579 <u><</u> 25,479   g 49,273 ☐ 49,723

a 32,003 ☐ 33,200   h 94,875 ☐ 95,874

b 54,920 ☐ 54,920   i 61,439 ☐ 16,439

c 14,019 ☐ 41,910   j 22,044 ☐ 22,440

d 37,249 ☐ 94,375   k 16,134 ☐ 16,134

e 93,002 ☐ 92,030   l 83,270 ☐ 83,720

f 72,490 ☐ 74,290   m 72,467 ☐ 72,467

2 Circle the correct answer.

35,284 is less than / is equal to / (is greater than) 34,582.

a 72,145 is less than / is equal to / is greater than 75,214.

b 42,957 is less than / is equal to / is greater than 24,957.

c 53,240 is less than / is equal to / is greater than 53,420.

d 17,490 is less than / is equal to / is greater than 17,490.

3 Write a number to make the following true.

43,245 > <u>15,256</u>   f 43,495 > _____

a 72,193 < _____   g 22,043 = _____

b 28,057 = _____   h 52,949 < _____

c 41,347 > _____   i 49,563 < _____

d 32,090 > _____   j 79,345 < _____

e 16,325 < _____   k 81,090 < _____

                              © Shell Education

ROUNDING TO 10,000

Rounding is useful when you need to estimate an answer.

Round-down numbers					Round-up numbers				
←									→
0	1	2	3	4	5	6	7	8	9

Rounding to 10,000

1 Go to the ten thousands column.

2 Write the round-up number above the ten thousands.

3 Circle the number in the thousands column.

4 Is it a round-up or round-down number?

5 Round your number.

> If the number is less than 5, you round down. If the number is 5 or more, you round up.

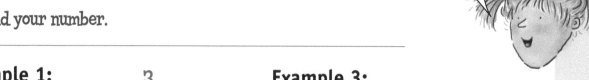

Example 1:
Round 24,358 to the nearest 10,000.

2④,358 ↶down
20,000

Example 2:
Round 36,529 to the nearest 10,000.

3⑥,529 ↖up
40,000

Example 3:
Round 15,372 to the nearest 10,000.   _____

_____

Example 4:
Round 89,647 to the nearest 10,000.   _____

_____

Your turn

Round these number to the nearest 10,000.

● 24,597   2④,597 ↶down
20,000

b 52,599   _____

_____

a 37,924   _____

c 75,023   _____

_____

SELF CHECK   Mark how you feel

Got it!	Need help...	I don't get it
☐	☐	☐

Check your answers
How many did you get correct?

PRACTICE

1 Round these numbers to the nearest 10,000.

⬤ 4⑤,926
  5

  _50,000_

a 36,439

_____

b 72,493

_____

c 55,386

_____

d 91,254

_____

e 82,649

_____

f 79,501

_____

g 86,255

_____

h 47,153

_____

2 Round the following.

⬤ 62,510

nearest 10	_62,510_
nearest 100	_62,600_
nearest 1,000	_63,000_
nearest 10,000	_60,000_

a 37,502

nearest 10   _____

nearest 100   _____

nearest 1,000   _____

nearest 10,000   _____

b 71,539

nearest 10   _____

nearest 100   _____

nearest 1,000   _____

nearest 10,000   _____

c 84,965

nearest 10   _____

nearest 100   _____

nearest 1,000   _____

nearest 10,000   _____

d 26,608

nearest 10   _____

nearest 100   _____

nearest 1,000   _____

nearest 10,000   _____

e 30,429

nearest 10   _____

nearest 100   _____

nearest 1,000   _____

nearest 10,000   _____

© Shell Education

1 Write the following numbers in words.

a 675 _____

b 429 _____

c 3,056 _____

d 2,350 _____

e 7,438 _____

f 8,503 _____

g 26,590

_____

h 37,429

_____

2 Complete the table.

	Number	Ten thousands	Thousands	Hundreds	Tens	Ones
a	79					
b	838					
c	903					
d	1,430					
e	2,574					
f	3,827					
g	12,507					
h	35,639					
i	40,256					
j	57,007					

REVIEW

3. Circle the numbers with eight hundreds.

836   4,798   3,863   12,484   983   842   29,836

5,815   183   98   28   3,683   19,837   2,862

4. Circle the numbers with four thousands.

24,293   94   47,473   2,414   4,684   8,436

2,594   4,004   499   94,362   4,937   34,876

5. What is the place value of the 6 in these numbers?

a   625_____

b   1,629 _____

c   6,384 _____

d   26,378 _____

e   64,321 _____

f   69,342 _____

g   16,373 _____

h   47,624 _____

i   56,290 _____

j   97,635 _____

k   24,376 _____

l   16 _____

m   25,960 _____

n   3,640 _____

o   74,362 _____

6. Write the numbers.

a   6 ten thousands, 3 hundreds, 4 ones = _____

b   8 thousands, 2 ten thousands, 1 ones, 3 tens = _____

c   7 tens, 4 hundreds, 8 ones = _____

d   5 thousands, 7 tens = _____

e   8 ten thousands, 6 tens, 3 ones = _____

f   3 thousands, 5 ten thousands, 2 ones = _____

g   8 ones, 6 tens, 4 ten thousands = _____

h   9 tens, 7 ten thousands, 5 hundreds = _____

     © Shell Education

7 What is the value of the 2 in these numbers?

a 423 _____   **g** 32 _____   **m** 72 _____

b 732 _____   **h** 24,358 _____   **n** 239 _____

c 729 _____   **i** 52,436 _____   **o** 2,993 _____

d 12 _____   **j** 57,230 _____   **p** 23,491 _____

e 2,495 _____   **k** 42,135 _____   **q** 62,410 _____

f 3,245 _____   **l** 29,693 _____   **r** 43,216 _____

8 Fill in the number expanders.

a 2,759

	thousands		hundreds		tens		ones

b 3,248

				ones

c 46,819

	ten thousands		thousands		hundreds		tens		ones

d 1,037

	thousands		hundreds		tens		ones

9 Write in expanded form.

a 632 = _____

b 207 = _____

c 910 = _____

d 1,438 = _____

e 3,589 = _____

f 7,136 = _____

REVIEW

10 Show these numbers on the abacuses.

a 3,942

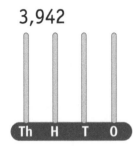

b 7,495

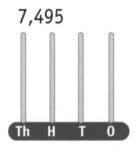

c 8,973

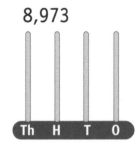

11 Write the correct symbol: >, <, or =.

a 347 ☐ 293

b 1,250 ☐ 1,205

c 7,646 ☐ 7,646

d 24,937 ☐ 29,473

e 8,932 ☐ 2,938

f 63,241 ☐ 61,243

g 11,345 ☐ 54,311

h 76,201 ☐ 72,106

i 13,254 ☐ 13,254

j 92,374 ☐ 97,234

k 84,921 ☐ 81,924

l 74,328 ☐ 83,274

12 Round the numbers to complete the table.

	Number	Nearest 10	Nearest 100	Nearest 1,000	Nearest 10,000
a	13,427				
b	49,238				
c	56,502				
d	60,348				
e	99,037				
f	74,295				
g	86,697				

© Shell Education

ADDITION WITHOUT REGROUPING

Addition is when two or more numbers are combined
to make one larger number.

Example 1: Add.

Tens	Ones
2	4
+ 1	5
3	9

Example 2: Add.

Tens	Ones
3	5
+ 2	3
5	8

Start at the ones
column and add.

Example 3: Add.

Tens	Ones
6	2
+ 3	5

Example 4: Add.

Tens	Ones
8	4
+ 1	3

Your turn

Solve.

●
Tens	Ones
4	3
+ 2	5
6	8

b
Tens	Ones
7	3
+ 1	5

d
Tens	Ones
8	6
+ 1	1

a
Tens	Ones
5	2
+ 4	0

c
Tens	Ones
6	1
+ 2	2

e
Tens	Ones
7	5
+ 2	3

SELF CHECK Mark how you feel
Got it! Need help... I don't get it

Check your answers
How many did
you get correct?

PRACTICE

1 Add these numbers.

	Tens	Ones
	5	3
+	4	1
	9	4

b

	Tens	Ones
	3	2
+	2	5

d

	Tens	Ones
	7	5
+	1	1

f

	Tens	Ones
	5	6
+	4	2

a

	Tens	Ones
	1	5
+	2	4

c

	Tens	Ones
	6	8
+	2	1

e

	Tens	Ones
	8	3
+		4

g

	Tens	Ones
	2	8
+	5	1

2 Add these numbers.

	Tens	Ones
	4	2
+	5	6
	9	8

e

	Tens	Ones
	5	6
+	2	1

j

	Tens	Ones
	6	3
+	2	5

o

	Tens	Ones
	4	5
+	5	0

a

	Tens	Ones
	3	5
+	5	1

f

	Tens	Ones
	4	7
+	4	1

k

	Tens	Ones
	5	3
+	3	5

p

	Tens	Ones
	3	6
+	3	1

b

	Tens	Ones
	2	4
+	5	5

g

	Tens	Ones
	3	0
+	6	5

l

	Tens	Ones
	3	1
+	2	1

q

	Tens	Ones
	4	7
+	3	2

c

	Tens	Ones
	3	7
+	4	2

h

	Tens	Ones
	4	7
+	3	2

m

	Tens	Ones
	5	4
+	4	3

r

	Tens	Ones
	5	9
+	4	0

d

	Tens	Ones
	4	3
+	5	3

i

	Tens	Ones
	3	7
+	1	0

n

	Tens	Ones
	7	3
+	1	3

s

	Tens	Ones
	9	3
+		2

© Shell Education

3 Fill in the missing numbers.

	Tens	Ones
	2	4
+	6	2
	8	6

b

	Tens	Ones
	6	8
+		
	9	9

d

	Tens	Ones
	7	2
+		
	9	5

f

	Tens	Ones
	3	0
+		
	5	7

a

	Tens	Ones
	4	1
+		
	9	3

c

	Tens	Ones
	5	3
+		
	9	8

e

	Tens	Ones
	2	1
+		
	4	1

g

	Tens	Ones
	4	9
+		
	6	9

4 Round each number to the nearest 10 to estimate an answer for these number sentences.

 | 53 | + | 27 | is about (80)

(50) (30)

a | 62 | + | 13 | is about ◯

b | 78 | + | 24 | is about ◯

c | 81 | + | 19 | is about ◯

d | 73 | + | 24 | is about ◯

e | 52 | + | 18 | is about ◯

f | 72 | + | 15 | is about ◯

g | 43 | + | 28 | is about ◯

h | 56 | + | 31 | is about ◯

i | 36 | + | 42 | is about ◯

j | 41 | + | 17 | is about ◯

k | 53 | + | 59 | is about ◯

© Shell Education

5 Solve these three-digit problems.

Hund	Tens	Ones
3	2	6
+ 2	4	3
5	6	9

c

Hund	Tens	Ones
1	7	0
+ 5	1	5

f

Hund	Tens	Ones
1	7	4
+ 5	2	0

a

Hund	Tens	Ones
8	1	5
+ 1	6	3

d

Hund	Tens	Ones
6	4	2
+ 3	4	5

g

Hund	Tens	Ones
1	3	8
+ 4	2	1

b

Hund	Tens	Ones
2	2	7
+ 7	5	2

e

Hund	Tens	Ones
7	2	3
+ 2	5	6

h

Hund	Tens	Ones
1	3	6
+ 8	5	2

 6 Fill in the missing numbers.

H	T	O
1	6	3
+ 3	2	4
4	8	7

b

H	T	O
6	2	4
+		
8	5	7

d

H	T	O
4	3	8
+		
5	5	9

a

H	T	O
3	1	0
+		
5	9	0

c

H	T	O
5	2	3
+		
7	5	4

e

H	T	O
4	2	6
+		
9	9	8

 7 Round each number to the nearest 10 to estimate an answer for these number sentences.

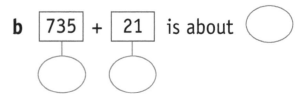

| 137 | + | 28 | is about | (170) |

(140)   (30)

b | 735 | + | 21 | is about | ( ) |

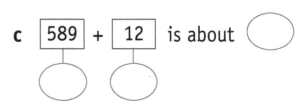

a | 256 | + | 17 | is about | ( ) |

c | 589 | + | 12 | is about | ( ) |

© Shell Education

ADDITION WITH REGROUPING

Addition is when two or more numbers are combined to make one larger number.

In addition, sometimes the sum of two digits in the same place value column is 10 or more.

Because there is only space for one digit, the 10 has to be regrouped into the next column.

SCAN to watch video

Example 1: Add.

Tens	Ones
¹7	5
+ 5	8
13	3

Example 3: Add.

Tens	Ones
¹1	5
+ 7	6
	1

Example 2: Add.

Tens	Ones
¹3	7
+ 5	9
9	8

Example 4: Add.

Tens	Ones
2	9
+ 8	3

Remember to regroup if you get 10 or more in a column.

Your turn

Add these numbers.

Tens	Ones
¹5	6
+ 4	9
10	5

a

Tens	Ones
7	8
+ 9	5

b

Tens	Ones
5	7
+ 3	4

c

Tens	Ones
6	2
+ 4	8

SELF CHECK   Mark how you feel

Got it!	Need help...	I don't get it
☐	☐	☐

Check your answers
How many did you get correct?

PRACTICE

 1 **Add these numbers.**

⬤
Tens	Ones
¹5	5
+ 4	9
10	4

b
Tens	Ones
8	7
+ 3	6

d
Tens	Ones
7	2
+ 1	9

f
Tens	Ones
8	4
+ 5	9

a
Tens	Ones
6	9
+ 4	5

c
Tens	Ones
4	7
+ 3	9

e
Tens	Ones
2	6
+ 3	5

g
Tens	Ones
9	3
+ 4	8

2 **Now try these.**

⬤
T	O
¹1	5
+ 6	5
8	O

e
T	O
7	2
+ 6	8

j
T	O
3	9
+ 7	2

o
T	O
5	5
+ 4	8

a
T	O
1	4
+ 5	6

f
T	O
5	4
+ 8	9

k
T	O
3	8
+ 9	4

p
T	O
3	6
+ 8	7

b
T	O
9	7
+ 2	3

g
T	O
3	9
+ 7	8

l
T	O
5	9
+ 2	5

q
T	O
9	4
+ 8	8

c
T	O
8	8
+ 3	9

h
T	O
4	8
+ 9	8

m
T	O
8	3
+ 1	7

r
T	O
5	4
+ 2	8

d
T	O
3	6
+ 9	7

i
T	O
8	9
+ 4	9

n
T	O
4	9
+ 2	5

s
T	O
1	7
+ 6	7

© Shell Education

3 Fill in the missing numbers.

(example)

T	O
¹5	6
+ 3	4
9	0

e

T	O
9	2
+	
13	0

j

T	O
5	8
+	
11	7

o

T	O
5	9
+	
12	4

a

T	O
7	7
+	
11	1

f

T	O
8	6
+	
13	1

k

T	O
2	9
+	
4	2

p

T	O
9	9
+	
14	5

b

T	O
8	4
+	
13	1

g

T	O
7	4
+	
14	1

l

T	O
1	9
+	
3	4

q

T	O
3	4
+	
9	2

c

T	O
9	6
+	
15	0

h

T	O
4	8
+	
13	4

m

T	O
3	5
+	
9	2

r

T	O
5	6
+	
11	1

d

T	O
5	8
+	
10	7

i

T	O
3	7
+	
6	2

n

T	O
4	7
+	
14	0

s

T	O
2	8
+	
6	4

4 Complete these three-digit problems.

(example)

H	T	O
¹4	¹7	3
+ 4	2	8
9	0	1

b

H	T	O
5	3	8
+ 4	5	2

d

H	T	O
4	9	3
+ 3	5	8

a

H	T	O
4	8	5
+ 2	7	6

c

H	T	O
2	8	7
+ 1	3	9

e

H	T	O
2	3	7
+ 4	5	9

f

H	T	O
8	4	5
+ 1	3	6

h

H	T	O
1	5	3
+ 3	2	9

j

H	T	O
6	2	4
+ 3	5	6

g

H	T	O
2	5	6
+ 6	8	9

i

H	T	O
2	5	8
+ 3	1	4

k

H	T	O
7	5	8
+ 1	4	3

 Fill in the missing numbers.

●

H	T	O
5	^{1}4	7
+ 3	0	7
8	5	4

e

H	T	O
3	8	9
+	1	
6	0	8

j

H	T	O
		9
+ 1	3	7
2	4	6

a

H	T	O
6	4	3
+		
8	5	2

f

H	T	O
4	2	8
+	4	
9	7	6

k

H	T	O
	8	
+ 6	5	7
8	4	3

b

H	T	O
8	2	6
+	3	
9	6	1

g

H	T	O
1	9	4
+	6	
9	6	3

l

H	T	O
		8
+ 1	4	7
6	7	5

c

H	T	O
7	4	4
+	1	
9	6	2

h

H	T	O
2	6	8
+ 3		
6	3	7

m

H	T	O
8	6	8
+	0	
9	7	4

d

H	T	O
5	2	9
+ 2		
7	4	7

i

H	T	O
6	3	2
+		8
9	3	0

n

H	T	O
3		
+ 5	1	7
8	8	4

© Shell Education

ADDITION REVIEW

1 Add these numbers.

a

T	O
5	7
+ 4	2

b

T	O
6	3
+ 3	1

c

T	O
5	8
+ 4	1

d

T	O
7	0
+ 2	9

e

H	T	O
3	0	8
+ 4	5	1

f

H	T	O
5	1	7
+ 3	8	1

g

H	T	O
4	2	3
+ 4	3	5

h

H	T	O
6	0	8
+ 3	9	1

i

H	T	O
2	7	3
+ 6	2	4

2 Add these numbers.

a

T	O
3	8
+ 6	9

b

T	O
7	6
+ 8	5

c

T	O
8	2
+ 5	9

d

H	T	O
3	7	2
+ 1	1	8

e

H	T	O
5	4	1
+ 2	3	9

f

H	T	O
6	7	5
+ 3	9	5

3 Fill in the missing numbers.

a

T	O
3	5
+	
5	9

b

T	O
4	2
+	
7	8

c

T	O
3	9
+	
8	4

REVIEW

d

T	O
7	6
+	
10	8

e

H	T	O
7	2	4
+		
9	8	6

f

H	T	O
5	9	7
+		
9	1	2

g

H	T	O
2	6	8
+		
7	9	5

h

H	T	O
+ 4	8	5
9	2	3

i

H	T	O
6	8	7
+	4	
8	3	6

4 Round each number to the nearest 10 to estimate an answer for each of these number sentences.

⬤ 54 + 28 is about (80)

50   30

a 62 + 33 is about ◯

b 87 + 42 is about ◯

c 37 + 42 is about ◯

d 25 + 81 is about ◯

e 371 + 83 is about ◯

f 652 + 19 is about ◯

g 537 + 29 is about ◯

h 586 + 21 is about ◯

i 746 + 52 is about ◯

© Shell Education

SUBTRACTION WITHOUT REGROUPING

An algorithm is a way of setting up a math question
to find the answer.

This is a subtraction algorithm:

Start at the ones column.

```
  5 8
- 3 2
-----
  2 6
```

Always subtract downward.

Example 1:

Start here.

Tens	Ones
7	3
− 1	2
6	1

Example 2:

Tens	Ones
8	5
− 3	3
5	2

Example 3:

Tens	Ones
9	8
− 3	4
6	4

Example 4:

Tens	Ones
6	4
− 3	2

Example 5:

Tens	Ones
7	7
− 4	6

Example 6:

Tens	Ones
8	3
− 5	0

Start at the ones
column and subtract.

Your turn

Subtract these numbers.

Tens	Ones
9	8
− 1	5
8	3

a

Tens	Ones
6	9
− 4	2

b

Tens	Ones
5	7
− 3	5

c

Tens	Ones
4	7
− 2	4

SELF CHECK Mark how you feel
Got it! | Need help... | I don't get it

Check your answers
How many did
you get correct?

PRACTICE

1 Subtract these numbers.

	Tens	Ones
	5	8
−	2	4
	3	4

b

Tens	Ones
5	7
− 4	1

d

Tens	Ones
4	6
− 2	4

f

Tens	Ones
3	9
− 2	0

a

Tens	Ones
6	9
− 3	7

c

Tens	Ones
3	8
− 1	7

e

Tens	Ones
4	3
− 1	1

g

Tens	Ones
2	6
− 1	5

2 Now subtract these numbers.

```
    9  8
 -  5  7
    4  1
```

b
```
    6  5
 -  4  2
```

d
```
    4  5
 -  3  2
```

f
```
    7  3
 -  5  1
```

a
```
    7  7
 -  4  2
```

c
```
    5  4
 -  2  0
```

e
```
    6  4
 -  3  1
```

g
```
    8  1
 -  3  0
```

3 This is Mario's math test. Find the answers to the questions, mark his test, and give him a score out of 8.

a
```
    2  4
 -  1  3
    1  1  ✓
```

c
```
    3  4
 -  1  2
    2  4
```

e
```
    9  3
 -  5  1
    4  2
```

g
```
    9  2
 -  8  0
    1  2
```

b
```
    7  2
 -  1  0
    6  1
```

d
```
    8  4
 -  2  0
    6  4
```

f
```
    8  7
 -  4  3
    4  4
```

h
```
    6  6
 -  2  4
    2  2
```

☐ out of 8

© Shell Education

SUBTRACTION WITHOUT REGROUPING AND THREE-DIGIT NUMBERS

This is a subtraction problem using a three-digit number.

1. Start at the ones column.
2. Then, go to the tens column.
3. Then, the hundreds column.

Hund	Tens	Ones
5	3	7
− 4	1	2

Always subtract downward.

Example 1:

Start here.

Hund	Tens	Ones
4	9	6
−	2	4
4	7	2

Example 2:

Hund	Tens	Ones
7	3	5
−	2	3
7	1	2

Example 3:

Hund	Tens	Ones
4	9	8
− 1	5	4
3	4	4

Example 4:

Hund	Tens	Ones
9	6	5
−	2	4
		1

Example 5:

Hund	Tens	Ones
4	9	6
− 1	0	3
		3

Example 6:

Hund	Tens	Ones
8	6	3
− 2	5	3
		0

First subtract the ones, then the tens, then the hundreds.

Subtract these numbers.

H	T	O
5	3	6
− 4	1	5
1	2	1

a

H	T	O
7	3	9
− 3	2	4

b

H	T	O
8	6	8
−	1	2

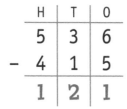

SELF CHECK Mark how you feel

Got it!	Need help...	I don't get it
☺ ☐	😐 ☐	☹ ☐

Check your answers
How many did you get correct?

PRACTICE

 1 Subtract these numbers.

```
      6 3 4        c    1 6 6       f    1 4 8       i    8 0 2
    -   2 3        -      3 2       -      3 2       -  4 0 1
    ─────────           ───────          ───────         ───────
      6 1 1
```

```
a   5 0 4          d   9 6 2        g   2 0 7        j   9 9 3
  - 1 0 2            -   4 1          - 1 0 7          - 8 1 2
  ─────────           ───────          ───────          ───────
```

```
b   6 3 5          e   7 5 3        h   8 7 1        k   4 6 8
  - 2 3 5            - 1 4 1          - 1 7 0          - 3 2 4
  ─────────          ─────────        ─────────        ─────────
```

 2 What is the difference between the numbers?

Numbers	Solutions		Numbers	Solutions
536 and 115	$\begin{array}{ccc} & 5 & 3 & 6 \\ - & 1 & 1 & 5 \\ \hline & 4 & 2 & 1 \end{array}$	d	897 and 881	
a 657 and 241		e	584 and 73	
b 773 and 252		f	779 and 779	
c 895 and 50		g	495 and 32	

 © Shell Education

SUBTRACTION WITH REGROUPING AND TWO-DIGIT NUMBERS

Here is a subtraction problem where we have to regroup from the tens column to help us solve the question.

SCAN to watch video

Tens	Ones
⁴5̶	¹3 ◄
− 2	8
2	5

We cannot take 8 away from 3, so we borrow from the tens column to make 13.

Example 1:

↰ Start here.

Tens	Ones
⁵6̶	¹2
− 3	6
2	6

Example 3:

Tens	Ones
⁷8̶	¹1
− 4	3

Example 2:

Tens	Ones
⁶7̶	¹4
− 3	5
3	9

Example 4:

Tens	Ones
5	3
− 2	4

Trade 1 ten for 10 ones.

Your turn

Use regrouping to subtract these numbers.

Tens	Ones
²3̶	¹2
− 1	5
1	7

a

Tens	Ones
5	8
− 3	9

b

Tens	Ones
9	1
− 7	3

c

Tens	Ones
7	1
− 2	6

SELF CHECK Mark how you feel

Got it!	Need help...	I don't get it
☺ ☐	😐 ☐	☹ ☐

Check your answers
How many did you get correct?

PRACTICE

1 Subtract these numbers.

Tens	Ones
⁴5̶	¹4
− 2	8
2	6

c

Tens	Ones
4	3
− 2	4

f

Tens	Ones
6	2
− 4	3

i

Tens	Ones
7	4
− 5	6

a

Tens	Ones
2	5
− 1	9

d

Tens	Ones
7	2
− 5	3

g

Tens	Ones
9	0
− 3	5

j

Tens	Ones
8	1
− 4	8

b

Tens	Ones
3	1
− 2	5

e

Tens	Ones
8	1
− 4	3

h

Tens	Ones
6	8
− 5	9

k

Tens	Ones
6	1
− 3	2

2 Subtract these numbers and then check your answers using addition.

Tens	Ones
⁴5̶	¹3
− 2	7
2	6

Tens	Ones
¹2	6
+ 2	7
5	3

c

Tens	Ones
9	3
− 6	4

Tens	Ones
+ 6	4

a

Tens	Ones
7	1
− 3	3

Tens	Ones
+ 3	3

d

Tens	Ones
4	1
− 2	5

Tens	Ones
+ 2	5

b

Tens	Ones
8	2
− 4	3

Tens	Ones
+ 4	3

e

Tens	Ones
6	0
− 3	4

Tens	Ones
+ 3	4

© Shell Education

SUBTRACTION WITH REGROUPING AND THREE-DIGIT NUMBERS

When the top number is too small, you must regroup.

Start at the ones column.

Hund	Tens	Ones
6	$^4\cancel{5}$	^{1}4
− 1	2	6
5	2	8

Always subtract downward.

Example 1:

Start here.

Hund	Tens	Ones
5	$^3\cancel{4}$	^{1}8
− 2	3	9
3	0	9

Example 3:

Hund	Tens	Ones
7	5	3
− 3	2	5

Example 2:

Regrouped twice.

Hund	Tens	Ones
$^3\cancel{4}$	$^{10}\cancel{1}$	^{1}5
− 1	3	6
2	7	9

Example 4:

Regrouped twice.

Hund	Tens	Ones
8	$^1\cancel{2}$	^{1}6
− 2	5	7

Trade 1 ten for 10 ones.

Trade 1 hundred for 10 tens.

Your turn

Use regrouping to complete these subtraction problems.

Hund	Tens	Ones
$^6\cancel{7}$	$^{10}\cancel{1}$	^{1}5
− 3	9	6
3	1	9

a

Hund	Tens	Ones
4	2	3
− 1	2	6

b

Hund	Tens	Ones
5	2	5
− 2	3	9

SELF CHECK Mark how you feel

Got it!	Need help...	I don't get it
😊 ☐	😐 ☐	😟 ☐

Check your answers
How many did you get correct?

PRACTICE

1 Subtract these numbers.

	Hund	Tens	Ones
	²3̸	¹¹2̸	¹4
−	1	5	8
	1	6	6

d

	Hund	Tens	Ones
	9	3	0
−	2	4	6

h

	Hund	Tens	Ones
	7	2	2
−	4	3	5

a

	Hund	Tens	Ones
	5	6	3
−	1	4	7

e

	Hund	Tens	Ones
	5	0	6
−	2	4	3

i

	Hund	Tens	Ones
	8	1	5
−	1	2	7

b

	Hund	Tens	Ones
	6	2	5
−	2	3	4

f

	Hund	Tens	Ones
	7	3	1
−	2	4	5

j

	Hund	Tens	Ones
	6	3	2
−	1	2	5

c

	Hund	Tens	Ones
	4	2	6
−	2	0	7

g

	Hund	Tens	Ones
	8	1	0
−	6	3	9

k

	Hund	Tens	Ones
	9	1	5
−	2	3	6

2 Subtract these numbers and then use addition to check your answers.

	H	T	O
	⁴5̸	¹1	9
−	1	3	3
	3	8	6

	H	T	O
	¹3	8	6
+	1	3	3
	5	1	9

c

	H	T	O
	9	1	3
−	4	2	5

	H	T	O
+	4	2	5

a

	H	T	O
	6	2	4
−	2	0	6

	H	T	O
+	2	0	6

d

	H	T	O
	8	4	4
−	3	5	6

	H	T	O
+	3	5	6

b

	H	T	O
	7	1	2
−	2	3	5

	H	T	O
+	2	3	5

e

	H	T	O
	4	0	9
−	1	2	3

	H	T	O
+	1	2	3

© Shell Education

SUBTRACTION WITH REGROUPING AND FOUR-DIGIT NUMBERS

Four-digit subtraction can also use regrouping.

Start at the ones column.

Always subtract downward.

Thou	Hund	Tens	Ones
3	³4̶	¹²3̶	¹2
− 1	3	5	7
2	0	7	5

SCAN to watch video

Example 1:

Thou	Hund	Tens	Ones
5	9	³4̶	¹2
− 1	4	2	3
4	5	1	9

Example 3:

Thou	Hund	Tens	Ones
6	⁷8̶	¹7	8
−		9	3

Example 2:

Thou	Hund	Tens	Ones
2	5	⁸9̶	¹3
−	2	8	7
2	3	0	6

Example 4:

Thou	Hund	Tens	Ones
9	0	3	0
− 5	8	2	7

Your turn

Use regrouping to complete these subtraction problems.

●
Thou	Hund	Tens	Ones
³4̶	⁹0̶	¹⁶6̶	9
− 3	8	7	8
	1	9	1

b
Thou	Hund	Tens	Ones
2	4	6	2
−	8	9	8

a
Thou	Hund	Tens	Ones
3	8	2	4
− 1	3	1	7

c
Thou	Hund	Tens	Ones
5	2	5	6
− 4	7	2	9

SELF CHECK   Mark how you feel
Got it!   Need help...   I don't get it

Check your answers
How many did you get correct?

PRACTICE

1 Subtract these numbers.

●
Thou	Hund	Tens	Ones
⁶7̶	¹¹2̶	¹⁸9̶	¹0
− 3	8	9	7
3	3	9	3

b
Thou	Hund	Tens	Ones
8	1	4	2
− 3	6	8	5

d
Thou	Hund	Tens	Ones
5	6	3	4
− 4	1	5	7

a
Thou	Hund	Tens	Ones
6	0	3	5
−	2	8	6

c
Thou	Hund	Tens	Ones
9	8	0	2
−	4	3	6

e
Thou	Hund	Tens	Ones
4	1	5	3
− 3	2	6	5

2 Subtract these numbers.

●
```
  ⁹1̶ 0 ¹3  6
-    3  4  2
   6  9  4
```

b
```
  5 0 3 5
- 4 1 9 3
```

d
```
  7 5 1 2
-     5 5
```

a
```
  7 1 3 2
-     4 9
```

c
```
  9 5 4 2
-   3 5 4
```

e
```
  3 2 1 7
- 1 2 8 9
```

3 Mark the following with ✓ if correct and ✗ if incorrect.

●
```
  5 6 ²3̶ ¹2
- 2 3 9  5
  3 3 7  7   ✗
```
Check:
```
  5 ⁵6̶ ¹²3̶ ¹2
- 2 3  9   5
  3 2  3   7
```

a
```
  8 ⁶7̶ ²3̶ ¹4
- 4 3  8  5
  4 3  6  9
```
Check:
```
  8 7 3 4
- 4 3 8 5
```

b
```
  ⁵6̶ ¹2 1 4
- 3  8  0 3
  2  4  1 1
```
Check:
```
  6 2 1 4
- 3 8 0 3
```

© Shell Education

ESTIMATING SUBTRACTION ANSWERS

Rounding can be used to get an answer close to the actual answer.

Example 1: Round each number to the nearest 10 before subtracting.

532 – 127 is about 400

530   130

Example 2: Round to the nearest 100 to estimate the answer.

973 – 141 is about ◯

◯   ◯

An estimate is near the answer, but it isn't perfectly accurate.

● Round to the nearest 10 to estimate the answer.

a

415 – 157 is about 260   613 – 419 is about ◯

420   160   ◯   ◯

● Round to the nearest 100 to estimate the answer.

a

323 – 167 is about 100   491 – 218 is about ◯

300   200   ◯   ◯

Your turn

SELF CHECK Mark how you feel

Got it!	Need help...	I don't get it

Check your answers
How many did you get correct?

PRACTICE

1 Round to the nearest 10 to estimate the answer.

| 523 | – | 416 | is about | 100 |

| 520 | | 420 |

a | 1,352 | – | 383 | is about |

b | 5,948 | – | 3,273 | is about |

c | 698 | – | 389 | is about |

d | 3,267 | – | 2,132 | is about |

e | 29,387 | – | 26,423 | is about |

f | 542 | – | 169 | is about |

g | 63,525 | – | 62,349 | is about |

 © Shell Education

2 Round to the nearest 100 to estimate the answer.

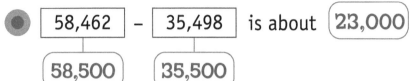

⬤ | 58,462 | – | 35,498 | is about | 23,000 |
| 58,500 | | 35,500 |

a | 7,389 | – | 4,214 | is about | ____ |

b | 51,752 | – | 34,635 | is about | ____ |

c | 569 | – | 317 | is about | ____ |

d | 4,382 | – | 1,216 | is about | ____ |

e | 24,362 | – | 19,431 | is about | ____ |

f | 893 | – | 179 | is about | ____ |

g | 4,373 | – | 2,536 | is about | ____ |

h | 6,136 | – | 5,988 | is about | ____ |

SUBTRACTION REVIEW

 1 Subtract.

a
```
   5 3
 - 2 1
```

d
```
   9 5
 - 4 3
```

g
```
   5 0
 - 3 6
```

j
```
   4 3 4
 - 1 2 3
```

b
```
   7 5
 - 1 3
```

e
```
   7 5
 - 3 8
```

h
```
   7 1
 - 5 4
```

k
```
   5 3 7
 - 2 4 8
```

c
```
   8 4
 - 2 2
```

f
```
   8 8
 - 6 9
```

i
```
   1 2 9
 -   1 8
```

l
```
   6 2 4
 -   3 5
```

2 Subtract.

a
```
   4 5 9 7
 - 2 1 3 2
```

c
```
   6 5 3 7
 - 4 2 1 5
```

e
```
   5 0 3 5
 -   2 5 6
```

b
```
   5 9 3 2
 -   4 5 1
```

d
```
   7 5 0 3
 - 1 2 8 5
```

f
```
   6 8 4 1
 -   2 3 0
```

3 Solve these problems and check your answers with addition.

a
```
   5 8
 - 3 2        + 3 2
```

c
```
   5 4 7
 - 1 2 3        + 1 2 3
```

b
```
   7 4
 - 2 5        + 2 5
```

d
```
   6 1 4
 - 2 5 3        + 2 5 3
```

© Shell Education

4 Solve these problems and check your answers with addition.

a
```
   4 3 5 7                    1 4 3
 -   1 4 3        +           1 4 3
 ─────────        ───────────────
```

b
```
   8 7 3 4                  2 3 0 5
 - 2 3 0 5        + 2 3 0 5
 ─────────        ───────────────
```

5 Hassan's test paper is shown. Check if his answers are correct. Put a check mark next to the correct answers and put an *X* next to the wrong ones. Give Hassan a final score out of 7.

a
```
   5 3
 - 1 4
 ─────
   4 1
```

b
```
   7 2
 - 5 1
 ─────
   2 1
```

c
```
   1 5 7
 -   4 8
 ───────
   1 1 1
```

d
```
   ⁵6̸ ¹0 3
 -   1 4 2
 ─────────
     4 6 1
```

e
```
   1 3 8 5
 -     7 3 5
 ───────────
   1 4 5 0
```

f
```
   4 ⁷8̸ ¹5 2
 - 1 0 7 1
 ───────────
   4 7 8 1
```

g
```
   5 9 8 2
 - 2 4 3 1
 ─────────
   3 5 5 1
```

☐ out of 7

REVIEW

6 Round to the nearest 10, then estimate the answer.

a | 529 | – | 137 | is about [ ]

[ ] [ ]

b | 324 | – | 213 | is about [ ]

[ ] [ ]

c | 3,521 | – | 2,989 | is about [ ]

[ ] [ ]

d | 7,436 | – | 4,321 | is about [ ]

[ ] [ ]

7 Round to the nearest 100, then estimate the answer.

a | 637 | – | 241 | is about [ ]

[ ] [ ]

b | 475 | – | 321 | is about [ ]

[ ] [ ]

c | 1,831 | – | 428 | is about [ ]

[ ] [ ]

d | 2,895 | – | 342 | is about [ ]

[ ] [ ]

© Shell Education

e 24,357 – 15,659 is about

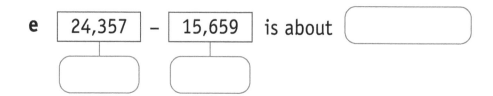

f 53,273 – 45,284 is about

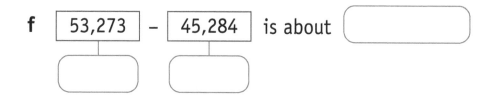

g 54,321 – 51,839 is about

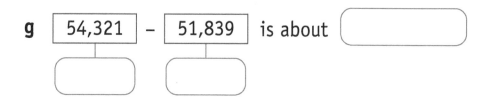

h 73,246 – 41,288 is about

GROUPS AND ROWS

Objects can be put in groups or rows to help solve multiplication problems.

Example 1:

2 rows of 5
These circles are in rows.
There are 2 rows of circles and 5 circles in each row.

Example 2:

3 groups of 4
These circles are in groups.
There are 3 groups of circles and 4 circles in each group.

Example 3:

_____ row of 6
These circles are in a row.
There is _____ row of circles and _____ circles in the row.

Example 4:

_____ groups of 5
These circles are in groups.
There are _____ groups of circles and _____ circles in each group.

Your turn

1 How many circles are in each row?

___3___ in each row

a

_____ in each row

b

_____ in each row

2 How many circles are in each group?

___4___ in each group

a

____ in each group

b

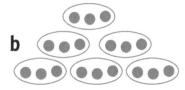

____ in each group

SELF CHECK Mark how you feel

Got it!	Need help...	I don't get it
😊 ☐	😐 ☐	😠 ☐

Check your answers
How many did you get correct?

© Shell Education

1 Draw circles to make each group equal.

 3 groups of 4

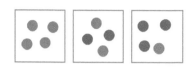

b 3 groups of 8

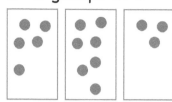

d 4 groups of 5

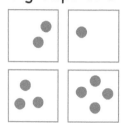

a 4 groups of 3

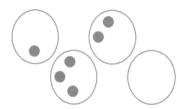

c 5 groups of 2

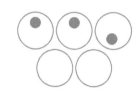

e 6 groups of 5

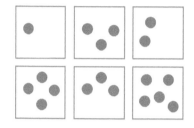

2 Make these rows equal.

● 4 rows of 3   **a** 5 rows of 4   **b** 3 rows of 6   **c** 2 rows of 7

3 Fill in the missing numbers.

<u>2</u> rows of <u>4</u>

a

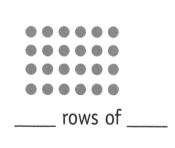

_____ rows of _____

b

_____ rows of _____

c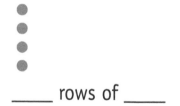

_____ rows of _____

d

_____ groups of _____

e

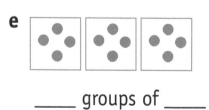

_____ groups of _____

f

_____ groups of _____

g

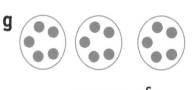

_____ groups of _____

h

_____ rows of _____

© Shell Education

REPEATED ADDITION TO SOLVE MULTIPLICATION

Multiplication problems can be solved using repeated addition.

Example 1:

3 rows of 4 = 12

4 + 4 + 4 = 12

3 × 4 = 12

Example 2:

3 groups of 6 = 18

6 + 6 + 6 = 18

3 × 6 = 18

Example 3:

4 groups of 5 = _____

5 + 5 + 5 + 5 = _____

4 × 5 = _____

Example 4:

_____ rows of 5 = 30

5 + 5 + 5 + 5 + 5 + 5 = _____

_____ × 5 = _____

Your turn

Fill in the missing numbers.

<u>2</u> rows of <u>5</u> = <u>10</u>

<u>5</u> + <u>5</u> = <u>10</u>

<u>2</u> × <u>5</u> = <u>10</u>

b

_____ rows of _____ = _____

_____ + _____ + _____ = _____

_____ × _____ = _____

a

_____ groups of _____ = _____

_____ + _____ + _____ = _____

_____ × _____ = _____

c

_____ group of _____ = _____

_____ = _____

_____ × _____ = _____

SELF CHECK Mark how you feel

Got it!	Need help...	I don't get it
☐	☐	☐

Check your answers
How many did you get correct?

© Shell Education

PRACTICE

PRACTICE

MULTIPLICATION

1 Draw rows or groups and fill in the blanks to show each problem .

● 3 rows of 4   **b** 3 rows of 3

3 rows of 4 = <u>12</u>   3 rows of 3 = ____

<u>4</u> + <u>4</u> + <u>4</u> = <u>12</u>   ____ + ____ + ____ = ____

<u>3</u> × <u>4</u> = 12   ____ × ____ = ____

a 5 groups of 1   **c** 8 groups of 2

5 groups of 1 = __   8 groups of 2 = ____

____ + ____ + ____ + ____ +   ____ + ____ + ____ + ____ +

____ = ____   ____ + ____

____ × ____ = ____   + ____ + ____ = ____

                        ____ × ____ = ____

2 Fill in the table.

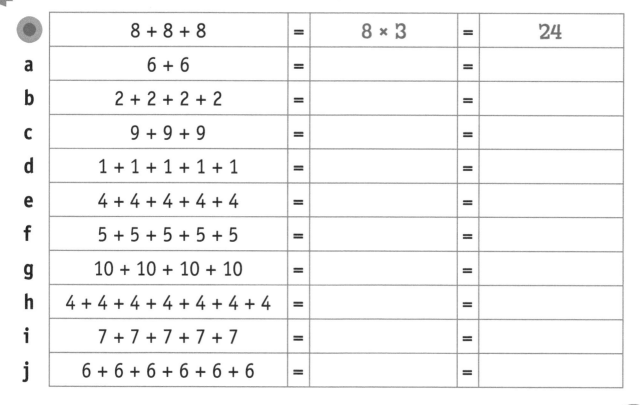

●	8 + 8 + 8	=	8 × 3	=	24
a	6 + 6	=		=	
b	2 + 2 + 2 + 2	=		=	
c	9 + 9 + 9	=		=	
d	1 + 1 + 1 + 1 + 1	=		=	
e	4 + 4 + 4 + 4 + 4	=		=	
f	5 + 5 + 5 + 5 + 5	=		=	
g	10 + 10 + 10 + 10	=		=	
h	4 + 4 + 4 + 4 + 4 + 4 + 4	=		=	
i	7 + 7 + 7 + 7 + 7	=		=	
j	6 + 6 + 6 + 6 + 6 + 6	=		=	

COMMUTATIVE PROPERTY

The commutative property of addition and multiplication means that the order of the numbers being added or multiplied can be changed and the answer is still the same.

Example 1:

4 + 3 = 7 | 3 + 4 = 7

Example 2:

2 × 8 = 16 | 8 × 2 = 16

Example 3:

5 + 8 + 1 = 14

1 + _____ + 5 = 14

8 + _____ + 1 = 14

Example 4:

4 × 3 = _____

_____ × _____ = _____

Your turn

Show each problem two ways.

• 3 × 4 = 4 × 3

a 6 + 3 = 3 + 6

b 2 + 4 + 8 = 8 + 2 + 4

c 5 × 2 = 2 × 5

d 3 × 7 = 7 × 3

e 5 + 3 + 2 = 2 + 3 + 5

SELF CHECK Mark how you feel

Got it! | Need help... | I don't get it

Check your answers
How many did you get correct?

© Shell Education

1 Complete the tables.

●	2 × 4 = 4 × 2		j	6 + 4 =
a	9 × 3 =		k	3 × 8 =
b	4 + 5 =		l	1 + 9 + 3 =
c	7 × 1 =		m	7 + 4 + 2 =
d	8 + 2 =		n	3 × 4 =
e	9 + 3 =		o	5 × 1 =
f	8 × 9 =		p	8 + 8 =
g	9 × 10 =		q	9 × 4 =
h	1 × 11 =		r	5 × 9 =
i	2 × 6 =		s	6 × 7 =

 2 Show each problem two ways.

● 3 × 2 = 2 × 3   **b** 3 + 2 = 2 + 3   **d** 5 + 4 = 4 + 5

Both equal __6__   Both equal ____   Both equal ____

a 7 × 4 = 4 × 7   **c** 9 × 3 = 3 × 9   **e** 6 × 3 = 3 × 6

Both equal ____   Both equal ____   Both equal ____

INVERSE OPERATIONS OF MULTIPLICATION AND DIVISION

Inverse means opposite. In math, × is the opposite of ÷. Multiplication is the inverse operation of division.

SCAN to watch video

$$30 \div 3 = \boxed{} \qquad \boxed{} = 10$$

$$3 \times \boxed{} = 30$$

Example 1:

The inverse of 15 ÷ 5 = 3 is 5 × 3 = 15.

Example 2:

The inverse of 4 × 3 = 12 is 12 ÷ 4 = 3.

> Multiplication is the inverse of division, and division is the inverse of multiplication.

Example 3:

The inverse of 35 ÷ 7 = 5 is 7 × _____ = 35.

Example 4:

The inverse of 6 × 10 = 60 is _____ ÷ 6 = _____.

Your turn

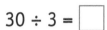

Fill in the missing numbers.

● 20 ÷ 4 = __5__

   4 × __5__ = 20

a 24 ÷ 6 = _____

   6 × _____ = 24

b 32 ÷ 8 = _____

   8 × _____ = 32

c 12 ÷ 3 = _____

   3 × _____ = 12

d 28 ÷ 7 = _____

   7 × _____ = 28

e 9 ÷ 3 = _____

   3 × _____ = 9

SELF CHECK Mark how you feel

Got it! | Need help... | I don't get it

Check your answers How many did you get correct?

PRACTICE

1 Match the inverse operations.

● $2 \times 4 = 8$ $21 \div 3 = 7$

a $5 \times 5 = 25$ $48 \div 4 = 12$

b $7 \times 3 = 21$ $9 \div 1 = 9$

c $10 \times 4 = 40$ $36 \div 6 = 6$

d $6 \times 6 = 36$ $40 \div 4 = 10$

e $9 \times 1 = 9$ $25 \div 5 = 5$

f $12 \times 4 = 48$ $8 \div 4 = 2$

g $3 \times 8 = 24$ $24 \div 8 = 3$

2 Complete the table.

	×	÷	×	÷
●	$3 \times 4 = 12$	$12 \div 4 = 3$	$4 \times 3 = 12$	$12 \div 3 = 4$
a	$6 \times 2 =$		$2 \times 6 =$	
b		$10 \div 5 = 2$		
c			$5 \times 8 =$	
d	$1 \times 7 =$			
e				$24 \div 2 =$
f			$5 \times 4 =$	
g	$7 \times 4 =$			
h		$32 \div 4 =$		
i				$33 \div 3 =$
j	$6 \times 7 =$			
k		$90 \div 10 =$		
l				$18 \div 9 =$

FACTORS AND MULTIPLES

Factors	**Multiples**
A factor is a number that divides another number evenly, with no remainder.	A multiple is the answer you get when you multiply two numbers together.

SCAN to watch video

3 and 4 are factors of 12. 12 is a multiple of 3 and 4.

3 × 4 = 12 ← multiple

factors

Example 1: What are the factors of 15?

1 × 15 = 15
3 × 5 = 15

15

1 3 5 15

1, 3, 5, and 15 are the factors of 15.

15 is a multiple of 1, 3, 5, and 15.

Example 2: What are the factors of 4?

4

1 2 4

1, 2, and 4 are the factors of 4.

4 is a multiple of 1, 2, and 4.

Example 3: What are the factors of 8?

8

1   8

Your turn

Write T for True or F for False.

● 4 is a factor of 20. __T__   c 2 is a factor of 4. ____

a A factor of 10 is 3. ____   d A multiple of 10 is 25. ____

b 50 is a multiple of 25. ____   e A factor of 50 is 5. ____

SELF CHECK   Mark how you feel
Got it!   Need help...   I don't get it

Check your answers
How many did you get correct?

© Shell Education

PRACTICE

1 Write the factors.

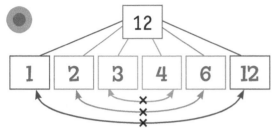

c

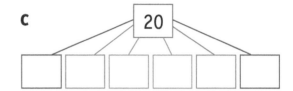

a

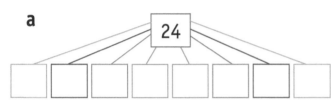

d

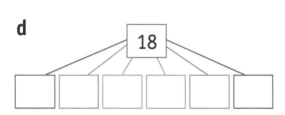

b

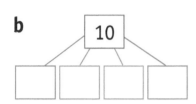

e

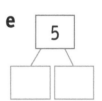

2 Write the first five multiples.

8: __8__, __16__, __24__, __32__, __40__

c 6: ___, ___, ___, ___, ___

a 4: ___, ___, ___, ___, ___

d 5: ___, ___, ___, ___, ___

b 7: ___, ___, ___, ___, ___

e 10: ___, ___, ___, ___, ___

3 Write in the missing factors.

3 × __4__ = 12   **c** 4 × ___ = 36   **f** ___ × 4 = 16   **i** ___ × 8 = 64

a 4 × ___ = 20   **d** 5 × ___ = 45   **g** 6 × ___ = 30   **j** ___ × 9 = 72

b ___ × 3 = 18   **e** 9 × ___ = 63   **h** 7 × ___ = 63   **k** 8 × ___ = 56

4 Complete the tables.

×	3	1	2	9	6	8
8	24	8	16	72	48	64

b

×	3	5	9	8	7	4
6						

a

×	2	5	7	8	3	9
7						

c

×	1	9	10	12	6	8
9						

MULTIPLYING TWO-DIGIT NUMBERS BY SINGLE-DIGIT NUMBERS

Here are three different ways to multiply two-digit numbers by single-digit numbers.

SCAN to watch video

Example 1: 13 × 9

Using known facts	Multiplying the tens and then the ones	Using an area model
13 × 9	13 × 9	13 × 9
10 × 10 = 130	= 9 tens + 9 threes	
130 – 13	= 90 + 27	
= 117	= 117	= 90 + 27
		= 117

Area model:

	10	3
9	90	27

Example 2: 15 × 8

Using known facts	Multiplying the tens and then the ones	Using an area model
15 × 8	15 × 8	15 × 8
10 × __ = 80	= __ tens + __ fives	
80 + __ + __ + __ + __ + __ (5 sets of 8)	= 80 + ____	
= ____	= ____	= 80 + ____
		= ____

Area model:

	10	5
8	80	

Your turn

Solve using the three different methods.

a 42 × 7

40 × 7 = _____

_____

_____

42 × 7

4 tens + _____

_____

_____

42 × 7

40	2

_____

_____

SELF CHECK   Mark how you feel

Got it!   Need help...   I don't get it

Check your answers
How many did you get correct?

PRACTICE

1 Solve using known facts.

● 27 × 4

  20 × 4 = 80

  80 + 4 + 4 + 4 + 4 + 4 + 4 + 4

  = 108

a 52 × 5

  _____

  _____

  = _____

b 19 × 6

  _____

  _____

  = _____

c 28 × 3

  _____

  _____

  = _____

d 97 × 4

  _____

  _____

  = _____

e 88 × 8

  _____

  _____

  = _____

f 34 × 7

  _____

  _____

  = _____

g 45 × 8

  _____

  _____

  = _____

2 Solve by multiplying the tens and then the ones.

● 23 × 9

  = 9 × 2 tens + 9 threes

  = 180 + 27

  = 207

a 58 × 4

  = _____

  = _____

  = _____

b 46 × 3

= _____

= _____

= _____

c 39 × 7

= _____

= _____

= _____

d 71 × 8

= _____

= _____

= _____

e 62 × 5

= _____

= _____

= _____

 Solve using area models.

 45 × 9

```
        40      5
      ┌──────┬──────┐
   9  │ 360  │  45  │
      └──────┴──────┘
```

= _360_ + _45_

= _405_

a 63 × 7

```
      ___    ___
   ┌──────┬──────┐
 __│      │      │
   └──────┴──────┘
```

= ____ + ____

= ____

b 92 × 6

```
      ___    ___
   ┌──────┬──────┐
 __│      │      │
   └──────┴──────┘
```

= ____ + ____

= ____

c 32 × 8

```
      ___    ___
   ┌──────┬──────┐
 __│      │      │
   └──────┴──────┘
```

= ____ + ____

= ____

d 19 × 4

```
      ___    ___
   ┌──────┬──────┐
 __│      │      │
   └──────┴──────┘
```

= ____ + ____

= ____

e 86 × 3

```
      ___    ___
   ┌──────┬──────┐
 __│      │      │
   └──────┴──────┘
```

= ____ + ____

= ____

© Shell Education

MULTIPLICATION REVIEW

1 Fill in the missing numbers.

a

_____ rows of _____

b

_____ groups of _____

c

_____ rows of _____

2 Complete.

a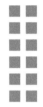

_____ rows of _____

_____ + _____ + _____ + _____ +

_____ + _____ = _____

_____ × _____ = _____

b

_____ groups of _____

_____ + _____ + _____ + _____ =

_____

_____ × _____ = _____

c

_____ rows of _____

_____ + _____ + _____ = _____

_____ × _____ = _____

d

_____ groups of _____

_____ + _____ + _____ + _____ =

_____

_____ × _____ = _____

3 Fill in the missing nmbers

a 8 + 8 + 8 + 8 = _____ × _____ = _____

b 5 + 5 + 5 + 5 + 5 = _____ × _____ = _____

c 6 + 6 + 6 + 6 = _____ × _____ = _____

d 2 + 2 + 2 + 2 + 2 + 2 = _____ × _____ = _____

e 1 + 1 + 1 + 1 = _____ × _____ = _____

f 9 + 9 + 9 + 9 + 9 + 9 = _____ × _____ = _____

REVIEW

4 Show each Commutative Property.

a 5 × 9 = _____ × _____

b 7 × 4 = _____ × _____

c 2 + 3 + 4 = _____ + _____ + _____

d 5 + 2 = _____ + _____

e 6 × 8 = _____ × _____

f 5 + 7 + 8 = _____ + _____ + _____

5 Complete these inverse operations.

a 4 × 9 = _____

 _____ ÷ 9 = _____

b 24 ÷ _____ = 8

 _____ × 8 = 24

c 5 × 6 = _____

 _____ ÷ 6 = _____

d 35 ÷ _____ = 5

 _____ × 5 = 35

e 42 ÷ _____ = 6

 _____ × 6 = 42

f 90 ÷ _____ = 9

 _____ × 9 = 90

g 8 × _____ = 32

 _____ ÷ 8 = 4

h 4 × _____ = 44

 44 ÷ _____ = 4

6 Write the factors.

a 12 _____

b 20 _____

c 36 _____

d 40 _____

7 Write T for True or F for False.

a 4 is a factor of 16. _____

b 20 is a multiple of 2. _____

c A factor of 30 is 6. _____

d 9 is a multiple of 28. _____

e 5 is a factor of 21. _____

f 60 is a multiple of 1. _____

g 20 is a factor of 40. _____

h A factor of 50 is 7. _____

  © Shell Education

8 Write the first 5 multiples.

a 9: _____, _____, _____, _____, _____

b 3: _____, _____, _____, _____, _____

c 10: _____, _____, _____, _____, _____

d 2: _____, _____, _____, _____, _____

e 1: _____, _____, _____, _____, _____

f 5: _____, _____, _____, _____, _____

9 Complete the tables.

a

×	1	6	3	8	11	4
5						
4						
7						
2						
9						

b

×	5	2	12	10	0	7
8						
3						
10						
1						
6						

REVIEW

 Solve.

a Use known facts

16 × 3

____ × ____ = ____

____ + ____ + ____ + ____ +

____ + ____

= ____

Multiply tens and then ones

16 × 3

= 3 × ____ tens + ____ sixes

= ____ + ____

= _____

Use an area model

16 × 3

	10	6
3		

= ____ + ____

= ____

b Use known facts

42 × 6

____ × ____ = ____

____ + ____

= ____

Multiply tens and then ones

42 × 6

= 6 × ____ tens + _____

= ____ + ____

= _____

Use an area model

42 × 6

= ____ + ____

= ____

© Shell Education

GROUPING

Grouping is sharing (or dividing) objects into groups of the same size.

Example 1: Share 12 balls among 6 children.

There will be **6** groups with **2** balls each.

12 ÷ 6 = 2

How many in each group

The number to be shared

The number of groups

Example 2: Share 16 balls among 4 children.

There will be **4** groups with **4** balls each.

_____ ÷ _____ = _____

How many in each group

The number to be shared

The number of groups

Your turn

Draw the ■, then complete the sentence.

● Share 15 ■ among 3 children.

Each child will get __5__ ■.

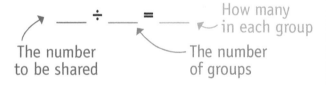

a Share 16 ■ among 8 children.

Each child will get _____ ■.

b Share 12 ■ among 4 children.

Each child will get _____ ■.

SELF CHECK   Mark how you feel

| Got it! | Need help... | I don't get it |

Check your answers
How many did you get correct?

PRACTICE

1 Complete the sentences.

There are _2_ equal groups with _3_ in each group.

a

There are _____ equal groups with _____ in each group.

b

There are _____ equal groups with _____ in each group.

c

There are _____ equal groups with _____ in each group.

d

There are _____ equal groups with _____ in each group.

2 Make equal groups, and then complete each number sentence.

● Groups of 2	**a** Groups of 4	**b** Groups of 3
 There are _5_ groups of 2. 10 ÷ _5_ = 2	 There are _____ groups of 4. 20 ÷ _____ = 4	 There are _____ groups of 3. 12 ÷ _____ = 3

3 Circle the groups, and then complete each number sentence.

● Groups of 5	**a** Groups of 6	**b** Groups of 7
 _15_ shared among _3_ equals 5.	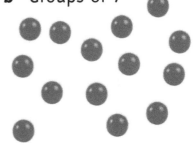 _____ shared among _____ equals 6.	_____ shared among _____ equals 7.

© Shell Education

EQUAL ROWS

An equal row is when the number in each row is the same.

Example 1:

Here are 20 counters.

 Now the 20 counters have been arranged in rows.

5 rows of 4

Example 2:

Here are 8 counters.

 Now the 8 counters have been arranged in rows.

4 rows of 2

Example 3:

Here are 15 counters.

 Now the 15 counters have been arranged in ____ rows of ____.

Each row has the same number of counters.

Your turn

Arrange the counters in rows.

● 6 counters

2 rows of 3

a 10 counters

5 rows of 2

b 8 counters

2 rows of 4

SELF CHECK   Mark how you feel

Got it!	Need help...	I don't get it
☺ ☐	😐 ☐	☹ ☐

Check your answers

How many did you get correct?

PRACTICE

 Draw ● in each box to show:

24 in 3 equal rows

3 rows of _8_ = 24

24 ÷ 3 = _8_

a 20 in 4 equal rows

4 rows of ____ = 20

20 ÷ 4 = ____

b 12 in 1 row

1 row of ____ = 12

12 ÷ 1 = ____

c 18 in 9 equal rows

9 rows of ____ = 18

18 ÷ 9 = ____

d 6 in 6 equal rows

6 rows of ____ = 6

6 ÷ 6 = ____

e 15 in 5 equal rows

5 rows of ____ = 15

15 ÷ 5 = ____

 Match each description to the right picture.

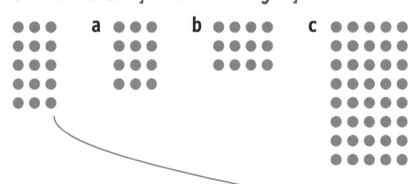

| 8 rows of 5 | 2 rows of 9 | 4 rows of 3 | 6 rows of 3 | 3 rows of 4 |

© Shell Education

REPEATED SUBTRACTION TO SOLVE DIVISION

One way division can be solved is by using repeated subtraction.

Example 1: Solve $24 \div 6$.

Start at 24

$24 - 6 = 18$
$18 - 6 = 12$
$12 - 6 = 6$
$6 - 6 = 0$

Keep taking away 6 until you get to 0.

4 times

so $24 \div 6 = 4$

Example 2: Solve $32 \div 8$.

Start at 32.

$32 - 8 = 24$
$24 - 8 = 16$
$16 - 8 = 8$
$8 - 8 = 0$

4 times

so $32 \div 8 = 4$

Example 3: Solve $18 \div 3$.

Start at ____.

____ − 3 = ____
____ − 3 = ____
____ − 3 = ____
____ − 3 = ____
____ − 3 = ____
____ − 3 = ____

☐ times

so $18 \div 3 = $ ___

Your turn

Complete these division problems.

$10 \div 5 = \underline{2}$

Start at 10

$10 - 5 = \underline{5}$
$\underline{5} - 5 = 0$

2

b $14 \div 7 = $ ____

Start at 14

$14 - 7 = $ ____
____ − 7 = ____

☐

a $9 \div 3 = $ ____

Start at 9

$9 - 3 = $ ____
____ − 3 = ____
____ − 3 = ____

☐

c $12 \div 4 = $ ____

Start at 12

$12 - 4 = $ ____
____ − 4 = ____
____ − 4 = ____

☐

SELF CHECK   Mark how you feel

Got it!	Need help...	I don't get it
☐	☐	☐

Check your answers
How many did you get correct?

PRACTICE

 Solve these division problems using repeated subtraction.

⦿ 21 ÷ 3 = _7_

Start at 21

21 − 3 = 18

18 − 3 = 15

15 − 3 = 12

12 − 3 = 9

9 − 3 = 6

6 − 3 = 3

3 − 3 = 0

a 45 ÷ 5 = ____

Start at 45

b 24 ÷ 8 = ____

Start at 24

c 30 ÷ 6 = ____

Start at 30

d 35 ÷ 7 = __

Start at 35

e 12 ÷ 2 = __

Start at 12

| 7 | times

[ ] times

[ ] times

[ ] times

[ ] times

[ ] times

© Shell Education

STANDARD ALGORITHM

Formal division is where division problems are written using the $\sqrt{}$ symbol instead of ÷.

SCAN to watch video

Example 1:

$$\begin{array}{r} 9 \\ 2\overline{)18} \end{array}$$

9 ← Answer (Quotient)

Number dividing by   Number being divided

You can use multiplication to check the answer:
2 × 9 = 18

Example 2:

$$\begin{array}{r} 12 \\ 3\overline{)36} \end{array}$$

Use multiplication to check your answer: 3 × 12 = 36

Example 3:

$$8\overline{)24}$$

Check using multiplication: 8 × ____ = ____

Your turn

Do the division, then check your answer with multiplication.

● $$\begin{array}{r} 8 \\ 2\overline{)16} \end{array}$$ Check: 2 × _8_ = 16

a $$6\overline{)36}$$ Check: 6 × ____ = 36

b $$7\overline{)42}$$ Check: 7 × ____ = 42

c $$9\overline{)81}$$ Check: 9 × ____ = 81

d $$4\overline{)48}$$ Check: 4 × ___ = 48

SELF CHECK Mark how you feel

Got it!	Need help...	I don't get it
☐	☐	☐

Check your answers
How many did you get correct?

PRACTICE

1 Solve the division problems.

$5\overline{)20}$ remainder 4

              d $9\overline{)90}$ h $8\overline{)64}$

a $10\overline{)40}$ e $4\overline{)36}$ i $4\overline{)20}$

b $3\overline{)33}$ f $7\overline{)63}$ j $3\overline{)21}$

c $7\overline{)56}$ g $8\overline{)56}$ k $5\overline{)30}$

2 Fill in the missing numbers, then check your answer with multiplication.

$6\overline{)30}$ remainder 5   Check: 6 × __5__ = 30   d $3\overline{)15}$ Check: 3 × ____ = 15

a $4\overline{)}$ remainder 7   Check: 4 × 7 = ____   e $9\overline{)45}$ Check: 9 × ____ = 45

b $7\overline{)56}$ Check: 7 × ____ = 56   f $2\overline{)}$ remainder 11   Check: 2 × 11 = ____

c $\overline{)60}$ remainder 10   Check: ____ × 10 = 60   g $5\overline{)}$ remainder 12   Check: 5 × 12 = ____

3 Write True or False.

$5\overline{)45}$ remainder 9   __True__   d $2\overline{)6}$ remainder 4   _____   h $3\overline{)36}$ remainder 12   _____

a $4\overline{)40}$ remainder 11   _____   e $2\overline{)8}$ remainder 6   _____   i $6\overline{)72}$ remainder 8   _____

b $5\overline{)60}$ remainder 12   _____   f $5\overline{)30}$ remainder 6   _____   j $7\overline{)49}$ remainder 7   _____

c $4\overline{)40}$ remainder 10   _____   g $10\overline{)12}$ remainder 2   _____   k $8\overline{)96}$ remainder 11   _____

 © Shell Education

DIVISION WITH REMAINDERS

When a number cannot be divided exactly, the leftover is called the remainder.

SCAN to watch video

Example 1:

I have 15 balls and share them equally among 4 people.

3 left over

Each person gets 3 balls.
There are 3 balls left over, and this is called the remainder.
So 15 ÷ 4 = 3 remainder 3.

Example 2:

I have _____ strawberries and share them equally between _____ people.

1 left over

Each person gets _____ strawberries and there is _____ left over.

The remainder is _____ strawberry.

So _____ ÷ _____ = _____ remainder _____.

Your turn

Share the objects equally.

● Share 10 balls among 4 people.

[   ] [   ] [   ] [   ]

Each person gets _2_ balls, and the remainder is _2_.

10 ÷ 4 = _2_ remainder _2_

a Share 12 balls among 5 people.

[   ] [   ] [   ] [   ] [   ]

Each person gets _____ balls, and the remainder is _____.

12 ÷ 5 = _____ remainder _____

SELF CHECK Mark how you feel

Got it!	Need help...	I don't get it

Check your answers
How many did you get correct?

© Shell Education

PRACTICE

1 Write the number sentence and the remainder.

● 13 apples shared equally among 5 people

　__13__ ÷ __5__ = __2__ remainder __3__

a 15 jelly beans shared equally among 2 people

　___ ÷ ___ = ___ remainder ___

b 18 balls shared equally among 4 people

　___ ÷ ___ = ___ remainder ___

c 48 bones shared equally among 8 dogs

　___ ÷ ___ = ___ remainder ___

d 25 fish shared equally among 3 seals

　___ ÷ ___ = ___ remainder ___

e 21 oranges shared equally among 7 people

　___ ÷ ___ = ___ remainder ___

f 29 chocolates shared equally among 4 children

　___ ÷ ___ = ___ remainder ___

g 83 balls shared equally among 9 people

　___ ÷ ___ = ___ remainder ___

2 Solve the division problems.

● 14 ÷ 3 = __4__ remainder __2__

a 22 ÷ 5 = ___ remainder ___

b 29 ÷ 3 = ___ remainder ___

c 43 ÷ 10 = ___ remainder ___

d 62 ÷ 12 = ___ remainder ___

e 83 ÷ 9 = ___ remainder ___

f 101 ÷ 10 = ___ remainder ___

g 146 ÷ 12 = ___ remainder ___

3 Match the problem with its remainder.

● 87 ÷ 9 = 9　　　　　　　remainder 2

a 93 ÷ 10 = 9　　　　　　remainder 1

b 27 ÷ 5 = 5　　　　　　　remainder 5

c 17 ÷ 2 = 8　　　　　　　remainder 6

d 64 ÷ 5 = 12　　　　　　remainder 4

e 47 ÷ 7 = 6　　　　　　　remainder 3

　　　　　　　　© Shell Education

DIVISION REVIEW

 Complete the statements.

a

There are _____ equal groups with _____ in each group.

b

There are _____ equal groups with _____ in each group.

c

There are _____ equal groups with _____ in each group.

 Circle equal groups, then complete the number sentences.

a Groups of 3

There are _____ groups of 3.

$15 \div \_\_\_\_ = 3$

b Groups of 5

There are _____ groups of 5.

$30 \div \_\_\_\_ = 5$

c Groups of 6

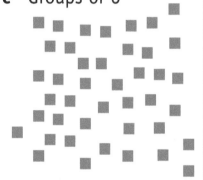

There are _____ groups of 6.

$42 \div \_\_\_\_ = 6$

 Draw ● in each box to show:

a 20 in 5 equal rows

5 rows of _____ = 20

$20 \div 5 = \_\_\_\_$

b 12 in 3 equal rows

3 rows of _____ = 12

$12 \div 3 = \_\_\_\_$

c 32 in 4 equal rows

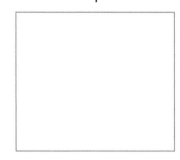

4 rows of _____ = 32

$32 \div 4 = \_\_\_\_$

REVIEW

4 Draw counters in:

   a 3 rows of 6   **b** 5 rows of 2   **c** 8 rows of 9

5 Use repeated subtraction to solve the division problems.

   a $32 \div 4 =$ _____

      Start at 32

   c $24 \div 6 =$ _____

      Start at 24

   b $48 \div 12 =$ _____

      Start at 48

   d $6 \div 6 =$ _____

      Start at 6

© Shell Education

6 Write one multiplication fact about each division problem.

a 30 ÷ 3

_____

b 72 ÷ 9

_____

c 80 ÷ 10

_____

d 40 ÷ 5

_____

e 24 ÷ 4

_____

f 21 ÷ 7

_____

g 64 ÷ 8

_____

h 20 ÷ 5

_____

i 12 ÷ 6

_____

j 36 ÷ 12

_____

 7 Write the correct numbers to complete the equations.

a ☐ ÷ 2 = 6

b ☐ ÷ 1 = 8

c ☐ ÷ 9 = 2

d ☐ ÷ 3 = 9

e ☐ ÷ 4 = 7

f ☐ ÷ 7 = 11

g ☐ ÷ 5 = 10

h ☐ ÷ 6 = 1

i ☐ ÷ 8 = 12

j ☐ ÷ 2 = 7

REVIEW

 8 Write the correct numbers to complete the equations.

a $42 \div \boxed{} = 7$ **f** $100 \div \boxed{} = 10$

b $33 \div \boxed{} = 11$ **g** $121 \div \boxed{} = 11$

c $24 \div \boxed{} = 3$ **h** $132 \div \boxed{} = 11$

d $64 \div \boxed{} = 8$ **i** $99 \div \boxed{} = 11$

e $72 \div \boxed{} = 8$ **j** $60 \div \boxed{} = 10$

 9 Solve these formal division questions.

a $3\overline{)36}$ **d** $6\overline{)42}$

b $5\overline{)20}$ **e** $6\overline{)48}$

c $4\overline{)32}$ **f** $2\overline{)24}$

 10 Fill in the missing numbers, then check your answer with multiplication.

a $6\overline{)24}$ Check: $6 \times \underline{\hspace{1cm}} = 24$ **f** $7\overline{)84}$ Check: $7 \times \underline{\hspace{1cm}} = 84$

b $\overset{12}{}\overline{)60}$ Check: $\underline{\hspace{1cm}} \times 12 = 60$ **g** $8\overline{)64}$ Check: $8 \times \underline{\hspace{1cm}} = 64$

c $8\overline{)56}$ Check: $8 \times \underline{\hspace{1cm}} = 56$ **h** $7\overline{)21}$ Check: $7 \times \underline{\hspace{1cm}} = 21$

d $4\overset{10}{\overline{)}}$ Check: $4 \times 10 = \underline{\hspace{1cm}}$ **i** $9\overset{11}{\overline{)}}$ Check: $9 \times 11 = \underline{\hspace{1cm}}$

e $\overset{6}{}\overline{)42}$ Check: $\underline{\hspace{1cm}} \times 6 = 42$ **j** $\overset{12}{}\overline{)72}$ Check: $\underline{\hspace{1cm}} \times 12 = 72$

 © Shell Education

Complete the number sentence and the remainder.

a 23 balls shared equally among 4 people

___ ÷ ___ = ___ remainder ___

b 37 fish shared equally among 12 people

___ ÷ ___ = ___ remainder ___

c 43 balls shared equally among 5 people

___ ÷ ___ = ___ remainder ___

d 92 candies shared equally among 10 people

___ ÷ ___ = ___ remainder ___

e 14 jelly beans shared equally among 7 people

___ ÷ ___ = ___ remainder ___

f 28 pens shared equally among 9 people

___ ÷ ___ = ___ remainder ___

g 63 pencils shared equally among 6 people

___ ÷ ___ = ___ remainder ___

h 48 flowers shared equally among 10 people

___ ÷ ___ = ___ remainder ___

i 25 jelly beans shared equally among 5 people

___ ÷ ___ = ___ remainder ___

j 59 marbles shared equally among 12 people

___ ÷ ___ = ___ remainder ___

12 **Solve the division problems.**

a 23 ÷ 4 = ____ remainder ____

b 28 ÷ 5 = ____ remainder ____

c 45 ÷ 6 = ____ remainder ____

d 62 ÷ 7 = ____ remainder ____

e 57 ÷ 11 = ____ remainder ____

f 133 ÷ 12 = ____ remainder ____

NUMERATORS AND DENOMINATORS

A fraction has two parts: the numerator and the denominator.

numerator
The top number in a fraction is the number of parts in this fraction.

$\frac{1}{4}$

denominator
The bottom number in a fraction is the total number of parts.

Example 1:
two-fifths = $\frac{2}{5}$

Example 2:
one-eighth = $\frac{1}{8}$

Example 3:
five-eighths = $\frac{5}{8}$

Remember, the larger the denominator, the smaller the parts.

Example 4:
one-quarter = $\frac{}{4}$

Example 5:
three-tenths = $\frac{3}{}$

Example 6:
_____-half = $\frac{1}{2}$

 Your turn

Trace the numerator red, the line green, and the denominator blue.

 $\frac{2}{5}$ c $\frac{1}{8}$ f $\frac{5}{8}$

a $\frac{1}{3}$ d $\frac{1}{2}$ g $\frac{2}{4}$

b $\frac{2}{8}$ e $\frac{7}{8}$ h $\frac{6}{8}$

SELF CHECK   Mark how you feel
Got it!   Need help...   I don't get it

Check your answers
How many did you get correct?

© Shell Education

PRACTICE

1 What is the numerator in these fractions?

⊙ $\frac{2}{8}$ 2   **b** $\frac{1}{5}$ ___   **d** $\frac{2}{2}$ ___   **f** $\frac{4}{8}$ ___

a $\frac{3}{4}$ ___   **c** $\frac{7}{8}$ ___   **e** $\frac{4}{5}$ ___   **g** $\frac{3}{5}$ ___

2 What is the denominator in these fractions?

⊙ $\frac{2}{5}$ 5   **b** $\frac{2}{4}$ ___   **d** $\frac{7}{8}$ ___   **f** $\frac{1}{4}$ ___

a $\frac{3}{8}$ ___   **c** $\frac{3}{5}$ ___   **e** $\frac{1}{2}$ ___   **g** $\frac{1}{5}$ ___

3 Write the name of the fraction.

⊙ $\frac{2}{5}$ is _two-fifths_   **e** $\frac{3}{4}$ is ___

a $\frac{3}{8}$ is ___   **f** $\frac{2}{4}$ is ___

b $\frac{1}{5}$ is ___   **g** $\frac{1}{8}$ is ___

c $\frac{7}{8}$ is ___   **h** $\frac{5}{8}$ is ___

d $\frac{3}{5}$ is ___   **i** $\frac{1}{3}$ is ___

4 Cross out the fraction with the different denominator.

⊙ $\frac{2}{5}$, $\frac{1}{5}$, $\frac{3}{5}$, $\frac{4}{10}$, $\frac{4}{5}$ **b** $\frac{1}{4}$, $\frac{2}{4}$, $\frac{4}{5}$, $\frac{3}{4}$, $\frac{4}{4}$ **d** $\frac{3}{5}$, $\frac{4}{10}$, $\frac{6}{10}$, $\frac{3}{10}$, $\frac{8}{10}$

a $\frac{1}{8}$, $\frac{3}{8}$, $\frac{7}{8}$, $\frac{4}{8}$, $\frac{3}{4}$ **c** $\frac{1}{3}$, $\frac{2}{3}$, $\frac{3}{3}$, $\frac{3}{8}$ **e** $\frac{2}{8}$, $\frac{3}{3}$, $\frac{6}{8}$, $\frac{5}{8}$, $\frac{8}{8}$

5 Write the name of each fraction you crossed out in Question 4.

⊙ _four-tenths_   **c** ___

a ___   **d** ___

b ___   **e** ___

© Shell Education   146435—Catch-Up Math

FRACTIONS—HALVES

Numbers that are parts of a whole are called fractions.
When there are two equal parts, each part is called one-half ($\frac{1}{2}$).

These objects have been divided into two equal parts.

These objects have NOT been divided into two equal parts.

Example 1:
Divide in half.

Example 3:
Divide into
two equal parts.

Example 2:
Divide into
halves.

Example 4:
Divide in half.

Your turn

Circle the shapes that have been divided into two equal parts.

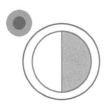 b   d   f   h

a   c   e   g   i

SELF CHECK   Mark how you feel

Got it!	Need help...	I don't get it
☐	☐	☐

Check your answers
How many did
you get correct?

PRACTICE

1 Mark the shapes that have been divided into two equal shares.

 ✓   **b**    **d**   **f**

a   **c**    **e**   **g**

2 Draw a line that divides each of the shapes in half.

    a   **b**   **c**

3 Label the shapes that have been cut in half ($\frac{1}{2}$). Cross out the shapes that have not been cut in half.

   **b**   **e**   **h**

    c    **f**    **i**

a   **d** 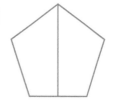   **g** 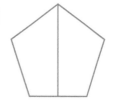   **j**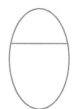

© Shell Education

FRACTIONS— QUARTERS AND EIGHTHS

When a whole is cut into four equal parts, each part is called one-quarter ($\frac{1}{4}$).

This square has been cut into 4 equal parts called quarters.

 One-quarter ($\frac{1}{4}$) of the square has been colored orange.

Example 1:
Color three-quarters ($\frac{3}{4}$).

Example 2:
Color two-quarters ($\frac{2}{4}$).

When a whole is cut into eight equal parts, each part is called one-eighth ($\frac{1}{8}$).

This square has been cut into 8 equal parts called eighths.

 One-eighth ($\frac{1}{8}$) of the square has been colored orange.

Example 3:
Color eight-eighths ($\frac{8}{8}$).

Example 4:
Color five-eighths ($\frac{5}{8}$).

Your turn

Circle in blue the shapes that are cut into quarters.
Circle in red the shapes that are cut into eighths.
Cross out any shapes that are not cut into quarters or eighths.

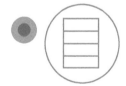 b d f

 a

 c  e g

SELF CHECK Mark how you feel

Got it!	Need help...	I don't get it

Check your answers
How many did you get correct?

© Shell Education

PRACTICE

1 Complete the table.

	Fraction name	Fraction	Picture
●	one-eighth	$\frac{1}{8}$	
a		$\frac{7}{8}$	
b	three-quarters		
c			
d	two-quarters		
e			
f		$\frac{4}{4}$	

2 Draw lines that divide each of these shapes into quarters.

 a ▢ b ⬭ c ▭

3 Draw lines that divide each of these shapes into eighths.

 a ▢ b ⬡ c ▭

4 Complete each fraction. Then, write the fractions in order from smallest to largest.

 $\frac{}{8}$ $\frac{}{4}$ $\frac{}{8}$ $\frac{}{8}$ $\frac{}{4}$ $\frac{}{4}$

_____ _____ _____ _____ _____ _____

FRACTIONS—THIRDS AND FIFTHS

When a whole is divided into three equal parts, each part is called one-third ($\frac{1}{3}$).

This rectangle has been cut into three equal parts.

When a whole is divided into five equal parts, each part is called one-fifth ($\frac{1}{5}$).

This rectangle has been cut into five equal parts.

Example 1:
Color two-thirds ($\frac{2}{3}$).

Example 3:
Color two-fifths ($\frac{2}{5}$).

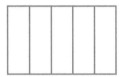

Example 2:
Color one-third ($\frac{1}{3}$).

Example 4:
Color one-fifth ($\frac{1}{5}$).

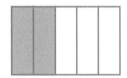

Your turn

Color with purple the shapes that have been cut into thirds.
Color with green the shapes that have been cut into fifths.
Cross out the shapes that have not been cut into thirds or fifths.

 b d f

a   c   e 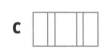 g

SELF CHECK Mark how you feel

Got it!   Need help...   I don't get it

Check your answers
How many did you get correct?

© Shell Education

PRACTICE

1 Complete the table.

Fraction name	Fraction	Picture
one-third	$\frac{1}{3}$	
two-fifths		
	$\frac{2}{3}$	
	$\frac{4}{5}$	
five-fifths		

2 Complete each fraction. Then, write the fractions in order from smallest to largest.

 $\overline{3}$ $\overline{5}$ $\overline{5}$ $\overline{3}$ $\overline{3}$ $\overline{5}$

_____   _____   _____   _____   _____   _____

3 What fraction is colored?

 $\frac{2}{3}$

b $\overline{}$

d $\overline{}$

a 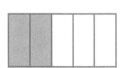 $\overline{}$

c 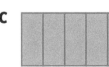 $\overline{}$

e $\overline{}$

© Shell Education   146435—Catch-Up Math   **117**

SIMPLIFYING FRACTIONS

SCAN to watch video

When you simplify a fraction, you make the numerator and denominator as small as possible.

When a fraction is written in its simplest form, the top and bottom numbers can no longer be divided by the same whole number exactly or evenly.

Example 1: Simplify $\frac{8}{12}$.

$\frac{8}{12} = \frac{2}{3}$

The 8 and the 12 are both divided by 4.

Example 3: Simplify $\frac{10}{24}$.

$\frac{10}{24} = \frac{5}{12}$

The 10 and the 24 are both divided by 2.

Example 2: Simplify $\frac{4}{8}$.

$\frac{4}{8} = \frac{2}{4} = \frac{1}{2}$

The 4 and 8 are both divided by 2 to give $\frac{2}{4}$ and then the 2 and 4 are divided again by 2.

Or you could just divide the 4 and 8 by 4 to get $\frac{1}{2}$!

Example 4: Simplify $\frac{6}{10}$.

$\frac{6}{10} = \frac{\ }{5}$

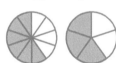

The 6 and 10 are both divided by ____.

Your turn

Simplify the fractions.

$\div 2$
$\frac{6}{8} = \frac{3}{4}$
$\div 2$

a $\div 2$
$\frac{8}{10} = \frac{4}{\ }$
$\div 2$

b $\div 10$
$\frac{30}{100} = \frac{\ }{10}$
$\div 10$

c $\div 5$
$\frac{10}{35} = \frac{\ }{\ }$
$\div 5$

SELF CHECK Mark how you feel
Got it! Need help... I don't get it
Check your answers How many did you get correct?

1 Fill in the missing numbers by simplifying the fractions.

Each bag has __4__ of the __32__ marbles, which is $\frac{1}{8}$.

a

Each bag has _____ of the _____ marbles, which is —.

b

Each bag has _____ of the _____ marbles, which is —.

c

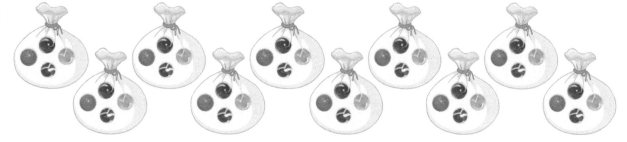

Each bag has _____ of the _____ marbles, which is —.

2 Simplify the fractions.

What number can BOTH
the numerator and the denominator
be divided by?

$$\overset{\div\ 8}{\underset{\div\ 8}{\frac{16}{24}}} = \frac{2}{3}$$

b $$\overset{\div\ \_\_}{\underset{\div\ \_\_}{\frac{9}{12}}} = —$$

d $$\overset{\div\ \_\_}{\underset{\div\ \_\_}{\frac{21}{28}}} = —$$

f $$\overset{\div\ \_\_}{\underset{\div\ \_\_}{\frac{24}{40}}} = —$$

a $$\overset{\div\ \_\_}{\underset{\div\ \_\_}{\frac{15}{20}}} = —$$

c $$\overset{\div\ \_\_}{\underset{\div\ \_\_}{\frac{50}{100}}} = —$$

e $$\overset{\div\ \_\_}{\underset{\div\ \_\_}{\frac{18}{30}}} = —$$

g $$\overset{\div\ \_\_}{\underset{\div\ \_\_}{\frac{40}{45}}} = —$$

COMPARING FRACTIONS

Comparing fractions means deciding which fraction is bigger and which fraction is smaller.

When the numerator is 1, the larger the denominator, the smaller the fraction.

1 whole									
$\frac{1}{2}$					$\frac{1}{2}$				
$\frac{1}{4}$		$\frac{1}{4}$		$\frac{1}{4}$		$\frac{1}{4}$			
$\frac{1}{8}$	$\frac{1}{8}$	$\frac{1}{8}$	$\frac{1}{8}$	$\frac{1}{8}$	$\frac{1}{8}$	$\frac{1}{8}$	$\frac{1}{8}$		
$\frac{1}{3}$		$\frac{1}{3}$		$\frac{1}{3}$					
$\frac{1}{5}$		$\frac{1}{5}$		$\frac{1}{5}$		$\frac{1}{5}$		$\frac{1}{5}$	
$\frac{1}{10}$	$\frac{1}{10}$	$\frac{1}{10}$	$\frac{1}{10}$	$\frac{1}{10}$	$\frac{1}{10}$	$\frac{1}{10}$	$\frac{1}{10}$	$\frac{1}{10}$	$\frac{1}{10}$

Sometimes fractions with different numbers are equal (equivalent).

Example 1: One-third ($\frac{1}{3}$) is larger than one-eighth ($\frac{1}{8}$).

Example 2: One-fifth ($\frac{1}{5}$) is smaller than one-half ($\frac{1}{2}$).

Example 3: Two-quarters ($\frac{2}{4}$) is equivalent to one-half ($\frac{1}{2}$).

Example 4: One-fifth ($\frac{1}{5}$) is bigger than _____ (−).

Your turn

Color and fill in the spaces.

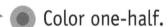

● Color one-half.

1 out of <u>2</u> = $\frac{1}{2}$

c Color one-third.

1 out of ____ = $\frac{1}{}$

a Color one-quarter.

1 out of ____ = $\frac{1}{}$

d Color one-fifth.

1 out of ____ = $\frac{1}{}$

SELF CHECK   Mark how you feel

Got it!	Need help...	I don't get it
☐	☐	☐

Check your answers
How many did you get correct?

PRACTICE

1 Number the boxes to order the fractions from largest (1) to smallest (6).

a

b

2 Write the correct symbol: >, <, or =

⦿ $\frac{1}{3}$ < $\frac{1}{2}$ **c** $\frac{1}{5}$ ☐ $\frac{1}{4}$ **f** $\frac{3}{5}$ ☐ $\frac{2}{3}$ **i** $\frac{3}{4}$ ☐ $\frac{6}{8}$

a $\frac{1}{2}$ ☐ $\frac{4}{8}$ **d** $\frac{2}{3}$ ☐ $\frac{1}{2}$ **g** $\frac{4}{5}$ ☐ $\frac{3}{4}$ **j** $\frac{1}{4}$ ☐ $\frac{1}{8}$

b $\frac{1}{3}$ ☐ $\frac{1}{5}$ **e** $\frac{2}{5}$ ☐ $\frac{3}{4}$ **h** $\frac{2}{4}$ ☐ $\frac{1}{2}$ **k** $\frac{3}{3}$ ☐ $\frac{5}{5}$

3 Draw a smaller fraction, then write the fraction in the box.

⦿   **a**   **b**   **c**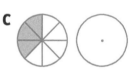

$\frac{1}{2}$ ☐ $\frac{1}{3}$ ☐ $\frac{1}{4}$ ☐ $\frac{3}{8}$ ☐

4 Draw a larger fraction, then write the fraction in the box.

⦿   **a**   **b**    **c**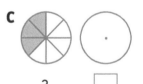

$\frac{1}{2}$ $\boxed{\frac{2}{3}}$ $\frac{1}{3}$ ☐ $\frac{1}{4}$ ☐ $\frac{3}{8}$ ☐

5 Draw a smaller fraction, then write the fraction in the box.

⦿   **a**    **b**    **c**

$\frac{2}{8}$ $\boxed{\frac{1}{8}}$ $\frac{3}{4}$ ☐ $\frac{1}{2}$ ☐ $\frac{2}{3}$ ☐

EQUIVALENT FRACTIONS

Equivalent means equal or the same.
Equivalent fractions are fractions that are equal to
or the same as each other.

$\frac{1}{4} = \frac{2}{8}$ One-quarter is equal to or the same as two-eighths.

To make equivalent fractions, you must multiply or divide both the numerator and denominator by the same number.

Example 1:

$\frac{1}{2} = \frac{2}{4}$ Both the 1 and the 2 in $\frac{1}{2}$ have been multiplied by 2.

Example 2:

$\frac{6}{8} = \frac{3}{4}$ Both the 6 and the 8 in $\frac{6}{8}$ have been divided by 2.

Example 3:

$\frac{10}{12} = \frac{}{6}$ Both the 10 and the 12 in $\frac{10}{12}$ have been divided by _____.

Your turn

Color the circle to show the fraction that is the same as the one on the left.

$\frac{3}{4}$ is equivalent to $\frac{6}{8}$

b

$\frac{1}{5}$ is equivalent to $\frac{}{10}$

a

$\frac{1}{2}$ is equivalent to $\frac{}{4}$

c

$\frac{2}{8}$ is equivalent to $\frac{}{4}$

SELF CHECK   Mark how you feel

Got it!	Need help...	I don't get it
☐	☐	☐

Check your answers
How many did
you get correct?

© Shell Education

PRACTICE

1 Color these shapes to show equivalent fractions.

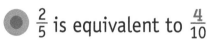 $\frac{2}{5}$ is equivalent to $\frac{4}{10}$

 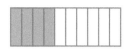

c $\frac{6}{10}$ is equivalent to $\frac{}{5}$

 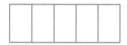

a $\frac{3}{4}$ is equivalent to $\frac{}{8}$

d $\frac{4}{8}$ is equivalent to $\frac{}{4}$

b $\frac{1}{2}$ is equivalent to $\frac{}{4}$

e $\frac{1}{4}$ is equivalent to $\frac{}{8}$

 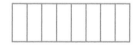

2 Create equivalent fractions.

 $\frac{3}{4} = \frac{6}{8}$ × 2

e $\frac{4}{8} = \frac{}{2}$ ÷ 4

j $\frac{1}{3} = \frac{}{6}$ × 2

o $\frac{3}{8} = \frac{}{24}$ × 3

a $\frac{1}{2} = \frac{}{4}$ × 2

f $\frac{2}{5} = \frac{}{10}$ × 2

k $\frac{1}{4} = \frac{}{20}$ × 5

p $\frac{4}{5} = \frac{}{30}$ × 6

b $\frac{3}{5} = \frac{6}{10}$ × 2

g $\frac{2}{4} = \frac{}{8}$ × 2

l $\frac{10}{15} = \frac{}{3}$ ÷ 5

q $\frac{20}{24} = \frac{}{6}$ ÷ 4

c $\frac{2}{8} = \frac{}{4}$ ÷ 2

h $\frac{1}{2} = \frac{}{8}$ × 4

m $\frac{3}{4} = \frac{}{12}$ × 3

r $\frac{18}{20} = \frac{}{10}$ ÷ 2

d $\frac{2}{3} = \frac{}{6}$ × 2

i $\frac{1}{4} = \frac{}{8}$ × 2

n $\frac{12}{16} = \frac{}{4}$ ÷ 4

s $\frac{12}{30} = \frac{}{10}$ ÷ 3

FRACTIONS REVIEW

 What is the numerator in these fractions?

     a $\frac{1}{3}$ __   **b** $\frac{2}{5}$ __   **c** $\frac{3}{4}$ __   **d** $\frac{2}{3}$ __   **e** $\frac{1}{4}$ __   **f** $\frac{3}{5}$ __

 What is the denominator in these fractions?

     a $\frac{2}{3}$ __   **b** $\frac{3}{8}$ __   **c** $\frac{7}{8}$ __   **d** $\frac{3}{4}$ __   **e** $\frac{2}{5}$ __   **f** $\frac{1}{2}$ __

 Write these fractions in words.

     a $\frac{3}{5}$ _____   **d** $\frac{1}{2}$ _____

     b $\frac{2}{8}$ _____   **e** $\frac{3}{4}$ _____

     c $\frac{4}{5}$ _____   **f** $\frac{7}{8}$ _____

 Draw a line that divides each shape in half.

     a   **b**   **c**   **d**   **e**

 Draw lines that divide these shapes into quarters.

     a   **b**   **c**   **d**   **e**

 © Shell Education

6 Circle the shapes that have been cut into eighths.

a   b   c   d   e

7 Circle with purple the shapes that have been cut into thirds and with green the shapes that have been cut into fifths.

a   b   c   d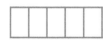

8 Write a smaller fraction.

a $\frac{7}{8}$ ___   c $\frac{1}{4}$ ___   e $\frac{2}{3}$ ___   g $\frac{3}{4}$ ___

b $\frac{1}{3}$ ___   d $\frac{3}{5}$ ___   f $\frac{4}{8}$ ___   h $\frac{1}{2}$ ___

9 Write a larger fraction.

a $\frac{6}{8}$ ___   c $\frac{3}{4}$ ___   e $\frac{1}{3}$ ___   g $\frac{1}{4}$ ___

b $\frac{2}{3}$ ___   d $\frac{2}{5}$ ___   f $\frac{5}{8}$ ___   h $\frac{4}{5}$ ___

10 Write the equivalent fraction.

a $\frac{3}{4} = \frac{}{8}$ d $\frac{2}{5} = \frac{}{10}$ g $\frac{8}{8} = \frac{}{4}$ j $\frac{1}{4} = \frac{}{8}$

b $\frac{4}{8} = \frac{}{4}$ e $\frac{1}{3} = \frac{}{6}$ h $\frac{3}{5} = \frac{}{10}$ k $\frac{4}{5} = \frac{}{10}$

c $\frac{2}{3} = \frac{}{6}$ f $\frac{1}{2} = \frac{}{8}$ i $\frac{1}{5} = \frac{}{10}$ l $\frac{1}{4} = \frac{}{8}$

DECIMALS TO HUNDREDTHS

 A decimal is part of a whole number. It is another way to write a fraction. This square is cut into hundredths (100 squares).

Each small square is one-hundredth of the whole.

The decimal 0.01 is one-hundredth ($\frac{1}{100}$).

Example 1:

3 hundredths

3 hundredths are colored.

$\frac{3}{100} = 0.03$

Example 2:

2 tenths

4 hundredths

24 hundredths are colored.

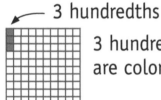

$\frac{24}{100} = 0.24$

Example 3:

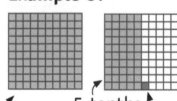

151 hundredths are colored.

5 tenths

1 whole   1 hundredth

$\frac{151}{100} = 1.51$

Example 4:

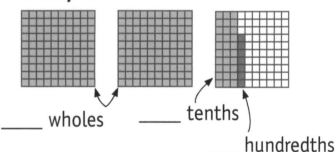

_____ wholes   _____ tenths

___ hundredths

_____ hundredths are colored.

$\overline{100} = \underline{\hspace{1cm}}.\underline{\hspace{1cm}}$

Your turn

What decimal has been colored?

    a   b   c

$= \frac{47}{100}$ $= \overline{100}$ $= \overline{100}$ $= \overline{100}$

$= 0.\underline{47}$ $= 0.\underline{\hspace{1cm}}$ $= 0.\underline{\hspace{1cm}}$ $= \underline{\hspace{1cm}}.\underline{\hspace{1cm}}$

SELF CHECK   Mark how you feel

Got it!	Need help...	I don't get it
☐	☐	☐

Check your answers

How many did you get correct?

PRACTICE

1 Color in the hundredths on the following squares.

34 hundredths   **b** 84 hundredths   **d** 172 hundredths

  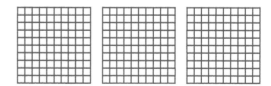

a 67 hundredths   **c** 12 hundredths   **e** 248 hundredths

2 Write the decimal for the shaded squares.

__2.10__

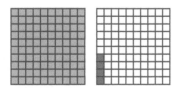

c _____

a _____

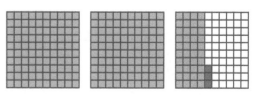

d _____

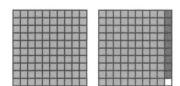

b _____

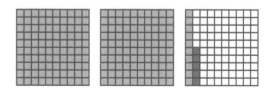

e _____

3 How many more hundredths need to be shaded to make one whole?

 Color __29__ to make one whole.

a Color ____ to make one whole.

b Color _____ to make one whole.

d Color _____ to make one whole.

c Color _____ to make one whole.

e Color _____ to make one whole.

4 How many hundredths need to be shaded to make two wholes?

● Color **169** to make two wholes.

g Color _____ to make two wholes.

a Color _____ to make two wholes.

h Color _____ to make two wholes.

b Color _____ to make two wholes.

i Color _____ to make two wholes.

c Color _____ to make two wholes.

j Color _____ to make two wholes.

d Color _____ to make two wholes.

k Color _____ to make two wholes.

e Color _____ to make two wholes.

l Color _____ to make two wholes.

f Color _____ to make two wholes.

m Color _____ to make two wholes.

© Shell Education

RELATING TENTHS TO HUNDREDTHS

These squares are cut into tenths.

Each has 10 equal parts, each worth $\frac{1}{10}$ = 0.10.

These squares are cut into hundredths.

There are 100 equal parts, each worth $\frac{1}{100}$ = 0.01.

SCAN to watch video

Example 1:

This square shows $\frac{2}{10}$ = 0.20

Example 3:

This is $\frac{20}{100}$ = 0.20

Example 2:

This square shows $\frac{7}{10}$ = 0._____

Example 4:

This is $\frac{70}{100}$ = 0._____

Here, one whole square and part of another square are colored.

Example 5:

This is $\frac{13}{10}$ = 1.30

Example 6:

This is $\frac{150}{100}$ = 1.50

Example 7:

This is $\frac{}{100}$ = _____

Your turn

What fraction is colored?

$\frac{4}{10}$ = 0.40

a

$\frac{}{10}$ = _____t

b

$\frac{}{100}$ = _____

c

$\frac{}{100}$ = _____

SELF CHECK   Mark how you feel

Got it!   Need help...   I don't get it

Check your answers

How many did you get correct?

PRACTICE

1 Shade and write the decimals.

  $\frac{2}{10}$

= _0.2_

a $\frac{7}{10}$

= ____

b $\frac{10}{10}$

= ____

2 Shade and write the decimals.

   $\frac{40}{100}$

= _0.40_

a $\frac{100}{100}$

= ____

b $\frac{30}{100}$

= ____

3 Complete the table.

	Words	Fraction	Decimal
	two-tenths	$\frac{2}{10}$	0.20
a	five-tenths		
b		$\frac{6}{10}$	
c		$\frac{10}{10}$	

4 Complete the following.

$\frac{3}{10} = \frac{30}{100}$

_3_ tenths = _30_ hundredths

b

$\overline{10} = \overline{100}$

__ tenths = ___ hundredths

a

$\overline{10} = \overline{100}$

__ tenths = ___ hundredths

c

$\overline{10} = \overline{100}$

__ tenths = ___ hundredths

© Shell Education

WRITING DECIMALS

SCAN to watch video

Fractions can be written as decimals.

The 0 in the ones position means
↓ there are no whole numbers.

Example 1: $\frac{24}{100}$ = 0.24 = 24 out of 100

two-tenths   four-hundredths

no whole numbers

Example 2: $\frac{70}{100}$ = 0.70 = 70 out of 100

seven-tenths   no hundredths

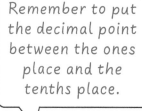

Remember to put the decimal point between the ones place and the tenths place.

The 1 in the ones position means
↓ there is 1 whole number.

Example 3: $\frac{137}{100}$ = 1.37 = 137 out of 100

three-tenths   seven-hundredths

The ___ in the ones position means
↓ there are 2 whole numbers.

Example 4: $\frac{249}{100}$ = ___.___ ___ = _____ out of 100

___ tenths   ___ hundredths

Your turn

Complete the table.

	Fraction	Decimal	Out of 100
●	$\frac{16}{100}$	0.16	<u>16</u> out of <u>100</u>
a	$\frac{28}{100}$		_____ out of _____
b			10 out of 100
c		0.93	_____ out of _____
d			312 out of 100

SELF CHECK   Mark how you feel

Got it!   Need help...   I don't get it

Check your answers
How many did you get correct?

PRACTICE

 Answer True or False.

⬤ 19 hundredths > 0.24 __False__

e 0.06 = 6 hundredths _____

a $\frac{72}{100} < \frac{198}{100}$ _____

f 7 hundredths > $\frac{70}{100}$ _____

b 0.34 = 34 hundredths _____

g 6.6 > $\frac{600}{100}$ _____

c $\frac{127}{100}$ = 172 hundredths _____

h 12.20 = $\frac{1220}{100}$ _____

d $\frac{23}{100}$ = 23 hundredths _____

i $\frac{40}{100} < 0.04$ _____

2 **Complete the table.**

Diagram	Fraction	Decimal
⬤	$\frac{69}{100}$	0.69
a	$\frac{281}{100}$	
b	$\frac{}{100}$	0.03
c	$\frac{}{100}$	

 Write the decimals.

⬤ $\frac{136}{100}$ = __1.36__

c $\frac{277}{100}$ = _____

f $\frac{8}{100}$ = _____

a $\frac{73}{100}$ = _____

d $\frac{403}{100}$ = _____

g $\frac{10}{100}$ = _____

b $\frac{14}{100}$ = _____

e $\frac{710}{100}$ = _____

h $\frac{983}{100}$ = _____

   © Shell Education

PLACE VALUE

Place value is the value of each digit in a number.
It means how much the digit is worth.

3 tens   2 ones   4 tenths   7 hundredths

32.47

Tens	Ones	Point	Tenths	Hundredths
3	2	.	4	7

Examples

Decimal	Hundreds	Tens	Ones	Point	Tenths	Hundredths
13.59		1	3	.	5	9
48.68		4		.	6	8
171.26	1		1	.	2	
257.99						

Your turn

1 Use blue to circle the tenths.

   36.3̇4̇   **a** 243.62   **b** 120.32   **c** 40.84

2 Use red to circle the hundredths.

   34.33̇   **a** 341.26   **b** 203.21   **c** 83.04

3 Use green to circle the ones.

   62̇.34   **a** 14.36   **b** 324.23   **c** 436.24

4 Use yellow to circle the tens.

   2̇9.23   **a** 70.34   **b** 123.58   **c** 542.63

SELF CHECK   Mark how you feel

Got it!	Need help...	I don't get it

Check your answers

How many did
you get correct?

PRACTICE

 Complete the table.

	Decimal	Tens	Ones	Point	Tenths	Hundredths
	17.42	1	7	.	4	2
a	63.81					
b	57.90					
c	40.75					
d	38.69					
e	94.21					
f	83.06					

 Trace the tens with yellow, the ones with green, the tenths with blue, and the hundredths with red.

36.24   **b** 47.36   **d** 83.95   **f** 92.72

a 13.09   **c** 72.09   **e** 57.60   **g** 64.58

 Place these decimals in ascending order.

2.73, 2.82, 2.14, 2.08, 2.37   2.08, 2.14, 2.37, 2.73, 2.82

a 5.05, 5.50, 5.15, 5.03, 5.58 _____

b 8.73, 8.30, 8.70, 8.37, 7.38 _____

c 9.16, 6.19, 9.61, 6.91, 19.6 _____

d 6.21, 12.62, 2.61, 1.26, 6.12 _____

e 7.57, 7.75, 5.75, 7.55, 5.57 _____

f 10.35, 10.53, 13.10, 13.35, 5.03 _____

g 1.23, 4.56, 7.89, 0.34, 1.07 _____

h 14.36, 14.96, 14.69, 16.34, 13.46 _____

    © Shell Education

DECIMALS REVIEW

1 Complete the fractions and decimals to match the shading.

a

$\overline{10}$ = 0.___

b

$\overline{100}$ = 0.___

c

__ = __.__

d

__ = __.___

e

__ = __.___

f

__ = __.__

g

__ = __.___

h

__ = __.__

2 Complete the fractions and decimals to match the shading.

a

__ __ = ____.____

b

__ __ = ____.____

3 How many more hundredths need to be shaded to make one whole?

a _____

b _____

c _____

d _____

REVIEW

4 How many more hundredths need to be shaded to make two wholes?

a _____

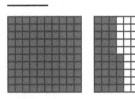

c _____

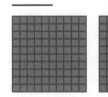

e _____

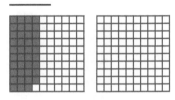

b _____

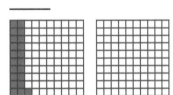

d _____

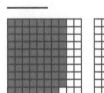

f _____

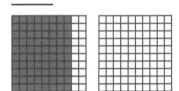

5 Complete the table.

	Colored Squares	Fraction	Decimal
a		$\frac{}{100}$	_____ . _____
b		$\frac{56}{100}$	_____ . _____
c		$\frac{}{100}$	2.29
d		$\frac{143}{100}$	_____ . _____
e		$\frac{}{100}$	_____ . _____
f		$\frac{}{100}$	_____ . _____

 © Shell Education

REVIEW

6 Write each fraction as a decimal.

a $\frac{127}{100}$ = _____   **c** $\frac{356}{100}$ = _____   **e** $\frac{495}{100}$ = _____   **g** $\frac{230}{100}$ = _____

b $\frac{73}{100}$ = _____   **d** $\frac{109}{100}$ = _____   **f** $\frac{9}{100}$ = _____   **h** $\frac{17}{100}$ = _____

7 Circle the tenths in the following.

    a 3.82   **b** 0.46   **c** 38.95   **d** 132.86   **e** 493.89

8 Circle the hundredths in the following.

    a 27.41   **b** 137.25   **c** 0.93   **d** 1.92   **e** 437.20

9 Circle the ones in the following.

    a 92.37   **b** 0.95   **c** 24.29   **d** 147.38   **e** 87.40

10 Circle the tens in the following.

    a 10.36   **b** 92.37   **c** 143.73   **d** 107.24   **e** 71.31

11 Place these decimals in ascending order.

    a 3.47, 7.43, 4.37, 7.34, 3.74   _____

    b 1.30, 1.03, 1.24, 1.68, 1.06   _____

    c 8.26, 6.28, 2.86, 8.62, 6.82   _____

PATTERNS

A pattern is when a sequence of objects, letters, or numbers is following a rule.

Object patterns

Example 1:

is repeated

Example 2:

is repeated

Example 3:

 is repeated

Example 4:

____ ____ ____ ____ is repeated

Number patterns

Example 5:
2, 4, 6, 8, 10, 12

Rule: + 2

Example 6:
5, 10, 15, 20, 25, 30

Rule: + 5

Example 7:
63, 54, 45, 36, 27, 18

Rule: – 9

Example 8:
27, 24, 21, 18, 15, 12

Rule: ____

Your turn

1 Complete these object patterns.

a ☐ △ ☐ △ ☐ ____ ____ ____ ____

b ○ ☐ ☆ ○ ☐ ☆ ____ ____ ____ ____ ____

2 Complete these number patterns and write the rule.

● 7, 14, 21, 28, _35_, _42_, _49_, _56_, _63_   Rule: _+ 7_

a 4, 8, 12, 16, ___, ___, ___, ___, ___   Rule: ____

b 110, 100, 90, 80, ___, ___, ___, ___, ___   Rule: ____

SELF CHECK Mark how you feel

Got it!	Need help...	I don't get it
☐	☐	☐

Check your answers
How many did you get correct?

PRACTICE

1 Complete the patterns and write the rule.

● 21, 19, 17, _15_, _13_, _11_   Rule: _− 2_

a 30, 25, 20, ___, ___, ___   Rule: ___

b 48, 44, 40, ___, ___, ___   Rule: ___

c 81, 72, 63, ___, ___, ___   Rule: ___

d 2, 4, 6, ___, ___, ___   Rule: ___

e 40, 50, 60, ___, ___, ___   Rule: ___

f 7, 17, 27, ___, ___, ___   Rule: ___

g 91, 81, 71, ___, ___, ___   Rule: ___

2 Continue these shape patterns.

c P A D P A ___ ___ ___ ___ ___

Write the missing numbers in the following patterns.

● 26, 28, _30_, _32_, 34, _36_   g 56, 63, ___, ___, 84, ___

a 12, 22, 32, ___, ___, ___   h 36, 30, ___, ___, 12, ___

b 90, ___, ___, 60, 50, ___   i 9, ___, 29, ___, 49, ___

c 12, 15, ___, ___, ___, 27   j ___, 16, 24, ___, ___, 48

d 14, ___, 24, ___, 34, ___   k 125, ___, 115, ___, 105, ___

e ___, 90, 85, ___, 75, ___   l 7, 12, ___, ___, 27, 32, ___

f ___, 75, ___, 71, 69, ___   m 4, 9, 14, ___, ___, ___

 Write the rule for each pattern.

● 160, 80, 40, 20   _Divide by 2_

a 46, 43, 40, 37   _____

b 18, 24, 30, 36   _____

c 93, 91, 89, 87   _____

d 4, 7, 10, 13, 16   _____

e 29, 25, 21, 17, 13   _____

f 163, 158, 153, 148, 143 _____

© Shell Education

Complete these object patterns.

a   ↑ ↓ ← → __ __ __ ← __ ↑ __ ← → __ __

b   X O Y P __ __ __ __ X __ Y __ __ O __ P X

c   △ ● ◗ __ ● __ △ __ ◗ __ __ __ △ ● ◗ __

d   ♥ ✗ ○ ♡ __ ✗ ○ __ __ ✗ __ ♡ ♥ ✗ __ __ ♥

e   ⊞ ⊓ ⊟ ⊠ __ __ __ ⊠ ⊞ __ __ __ ⊞ ⊓ __

f   ◐ ⊖ ⊗ ⊕ ◑ __ __ __ __ ⊖ ⊗ __ __ __ __

g   B A ■ ● B __ __ ● B __ ■ ● __ A __ __ __ A ■

h   4 5 7 9 __ __ 7 9 __ 5 __ 9 4 __ __ __ __ 5 7 __ __ __ 7 9

Complete the patterns.

a B, A, ☆, B, A, ___, ___, ___, ___

b ♡, ○, □, ♡, ○, ___, ___, ___, ___

c ○, ○, △, ○, ○, ___, ___, ___, ___

d ○, ◊, △, ○, ◊, ___, ___, ___, ___

e 8, 16, 24, 32, ___, ___, ___, ___

f 100, 90, 80, 70, ___, ___, ___, ___

g 42, 36, 30, 24, ___, ___, ___, ___

h 27, 36, 45, 54, ___, ___, ___, ___

 Write the missing numbers in the following patterns.

a 5, 10, ___, ___, ___, 30, 35

b 8, 18, ___, ___, ___, 58, 68

c 6, 11, 16, ___, ___, 31, ___

d 7, 16, ___, ___, 43, ___, 61

e ___, 100, ___, 80, 70, ___, 50

f 83, 79, ___, 71, 67, ___, ___

g 130, ___, 122, ___, 114, ___

h 96, ___, ___, 66, 56, ___, 36

3 Write the rule for each pattern.

a 5, 8, 11, 14, 17 _____

b 91, 87, 83, 79, 75 _____

c 4, 6, 8, 10, 12 _____

d 47, 42, 37, 32, 27 _____

e 18, 25, 32, 39, 46 _____

f 176, 170, 164, 158, 152 _____

g 3, 11, 19, 27, 35 _____

h 115, 105, 95, 85, 75 _____

METERS AND FEET

SCAN to watch video

A meter (m) is a unit of measurement used to measure big things. One meter is 100 centimeters (cm). A foot (ft.) is also a unit of measurement. One foot is 12 inches (in.).

These things can be measured in meters or feet.

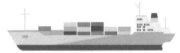  

| 1 m | 100 cm |
| 1 ft. | 12 in. |

We multiply to convert from a larger unit to a smaller unit.

Since 1 m = 100 cm, then 3 m = 300 cm.
3 m x 100 (number of cm in a m) = 300 cm

Since 1 ft. = 12 in., then 3 ft. = 36 in.
3 ft. x 12 (number of in. in a ft.) = 36 in.

We divide to convert from a smaller unit to a larger unit.

Since 100 cm = 1 m, then 500 cm = 5 m
500 cm ÷ 100 (number of cm in a m) = 5 m

Since 12 in. = 1 ft., then 60 in. = 5 ft.
60 in. ÷ 12 (number of in. in a ft.) = 5 ft.

Examples: Convert the measurements.

● 4 m = 400 cm   **c** 72 in. = _____ ft.   **f** 95 m = _____ cm

a 2 ft. = _____ in.   **d** 750 cm = ___ m   **g** 24 in. = _____ ft.

b 600 cm = ___ m   **e** 4 ft. = _____ in.   **h** 7 m = _____ cm

Your turn

List five different items that would be best measured in meters or feet.

● _____ a car _____   • _____

• _____   • _____

                                • _____

SELF CHECK   Mark how you feel

| Got it! | Need help... | I don't get it |

Check your answers
How many did you get correct?

                    © Shell Education

PRACTICE

1 Complete the tables.

	Centimeters	Meters
●	300 cm	3 m
a	100 cm	
b	500 cm	
c	700 cm	

	Centimeters	Meters
d		4 m
e		10 m
f		8 m
g		2 m

2 Complete the tables.

	Inches	Feet
●	24 in.	2 ft.
a	60 in.	
b	96 in.	
c	144 in.	

	Inches	Feet
d		7 ft.
e		4 ft.
f		3 ft.
g		10 ft.

3 Check the items that would be best measured in feet or meters.

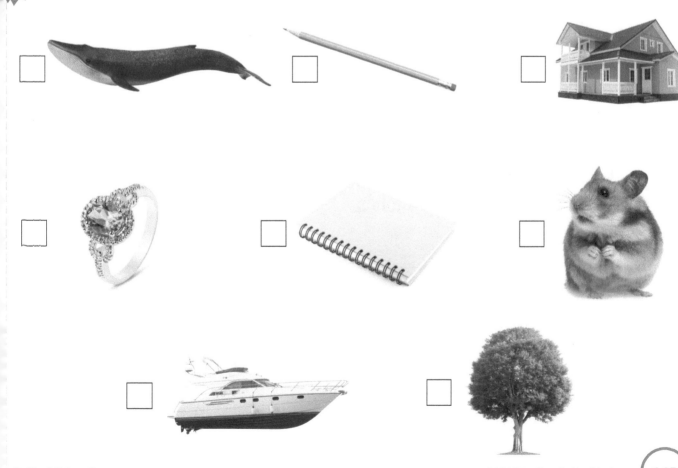

CENTIMETERS AND INCHES

A centimeter is smaller than a meter. It is used to measure smaller things. The symbol for centimeters is cm. An inch is smaller than a foot. It is also used to measure smaller things. The symbol for inches is in. When measuring with a ruler, always line the object up with the O.

SCAN to watch video

This ruler is 10 centimeters (10 cm) long.

This is 1 cm.

0 CM 1 2 3 4 5 6 7 8 9 10

This ruler is 6 inches (6 in.) long.

This is 1 in.

INCH 1 2 3 4 5 6

There are 100 cm in 1 m.

There are 12 in. in 1 ft.

Examples: Color the boxes next to the items that would be best measured in centimeters or inches.

a ■ a journal   d ☐ a car   g ☐ a hand

b ☐ a teacher's desk   e ☐ a book cover   h ☐ a truck

c ☐ a pencil   f ☐ a bed   i ☐ a toy car

Your turn

Name six different things that would be best measured in centimeters or inches.

• ___your finger___   • _____

• _____   • _____

• _____   • _____

SELF CHECK Mark how you feel

Got it!	Need help...	I don't get it
☐	☐	☐

Check your answers
How many did you get correct?

                    © Shell Education

PRACTICE

1 This ruler is 15 cm long. Use it to measure the lengths of the pencils.

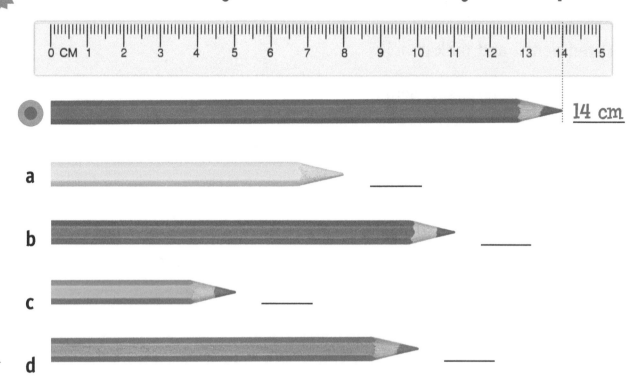

14 cm

a _____

b _____

c _____

d _____

2 Use the pencils above to complete the following.

a In the space above, draw a pencil that is 9 cm long. Color it purple.

b What color pencil is shortest?   _____

c What color pencil is longest?   _____

3 Order the pencils from shortest (1) to longest (6).

1 _green 5 cm_ , 2 _____ , 3 _____ ,

4 _____ , 5 _____ , 6 _____

4 What is the difference in length?

   a red pencil and yellow pencil   _____

   b red pencil and pink pencil   _____

   c red pencil and green pencil   _____

   d red pencil and orange pencil   _____

   e red pencil and purple pencil   _____

5 Draw lines of these lengths.
Remember to start measuring from the 0 on the ruler.

   ● two centimeters   ×———

   a five centimeters   ×

   b ten centimeters   ×

   c four and a half centimeters   ×

   d one and a half centimeters   ×

6 Measure the lines, and write the length in inches.

   ●   3 in.   _____

   a _____   _____

   b _____   _____

   c _____   _____

   d _____   _____

   e _____   _____

   f _____   _____

MILLIMETERS AND QUARTER-INCHES

Millimeters and fractional inches are used to measure small lengths. One millimeter is smaller than a centimeter. The symbol for millimeters is mm.
Inches can be broken down into half- and quarter-inches. They are written as $\frac{1}{2}$ in., $\frac{1}{4}$ in., and $\frac{3}{4}$ in.

SCAN to watch video

The small marks on the ruler are millimeters.

This line is 26 mm.

The small marks on the ruler are $\frac{1}{16}$ in.

There are 10 mm in 1 cm.

This line is $2\frac{1}{2}$ in.

Examples: Write the measurements marked on the ruler.

a <u>14</u> mm   **b** ____ mm   **c** ____ mm   **d** ____ mm   **e** ____ mm

Your turn

Mark and label these measurements on the ruler.

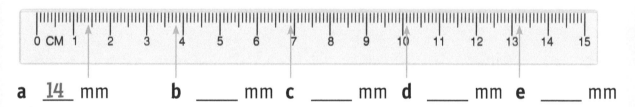

● $4\frac{1}{4}$ in.   **b** $3\frac{1}{2}$ in.   **d** $3\frac{3}{4}$ in.

a 2 in.   **c** 6 in.   **e** $5\frac{1}{2}$ in.

SELF CHECK Mark how you feel

Got it!	Need help...	I don't get it

Check your answers
How many did you get correct?

© Shell Education

PRACTICE

 1 Measure these lengths in millimeters.

● <u>67</u> mm _____

a ____ mm _____

b ____ mm _____

c ____ mm _____

 2 Measure these lengths in inches.

● <u>4.5</u> in. _____

a _____ in. _____

b _____ in. _____

c _____ in. _____

 3 Use the creatures and the ruler to complete the following.

a Write the length in millimeters beside each creature.

b Order the creatures from shortest to longest.

B			

c What is the difference in length for creatures D and C? _____

d What is the difference in length for creatures B and A? _____

A

B

C

D

© Shell Education

PERIMETER

Perimeter is the distance around a shape.
The symbol for perimeter is P.
To find the perimeter, add the lengths of all the sides.

SCAN to watch video

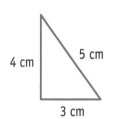

Perimeter = 3 cm + 4 cm + 5 cm
P = 12 cm
The perimeter (P) of the triangle is 12 cm.

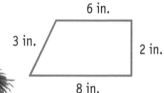

Perimeter = 3 in. + 6 in. + 2 in. + 8 in.
P = 19 in.
The perimeter (P) of the trapezoid is 19 in.

Examples: Find the perimeters.

Not all the sides are labeled. Use what you know about shapes to find the other lengths.

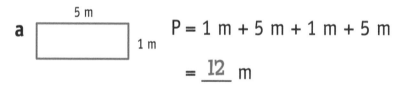

a

P = 1 m + 5 m + 1 m + 5 m
= __12__ m

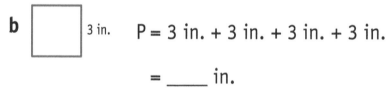

b

P = 3 in. + 3 in. + 3 in. + 3 in.
= ____ in.

Your turn

Calculate the perimeters.

P = __3__ + __4__ + __3__ + __4__
= __14__ cm

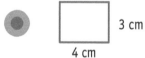

a

P = ____ + ____ + ____ + ____
= ____ m

b

P = ____ + ____ + ____ + ____
= ____ in.

SELF CHECK   Mark how you feel

Got it!   Need help...   I don't get it

Check your answers
How many did you get correct?

PRACTICE

 Add the side lengths to find the perimeter.

⦿ [square 4 cm] P = <u>4 cm + 4 cm + 4 cm + 4 cm</u>

= <u>16 cm</u>

a  2 in.   P = _____

= _____

b [hexagon] 3 mm   P = _____

= _____

c 1 ft. [octagon]   P = _____

= _____

d 3 cm [rectangle] 2 cm   P = _____

= _____

e 2 cm / 2 cm, 2 cm | 2 cm, 3 cm   P = _____

= _____

f 3 yd. [parallelogram]   P = _____

= _____

g 4 in. [parallelogram] 2 in.   P = _____

= _____

© Shell Education

LENGTH REVIEW

1 Write the missing words.

a One foot is equal to _____ inches. The symbol for foot is _____.

b One meter is equal to _____ centimeters. The symbol for meter is _____.

2 Name five items that could be measured in meters or feet.

_____

_____

_____

_____

_____

3 Complete the tables.

	Centimeters	Meters
a	100 cm	
b	300 cm	
c		5 m
d	600 cm	
e		8 m
f		2 m

	Inches	Feet
a	24 in.	
b		5 ft.
c		7 ft.
d	36 in.	
e	48 in.	
f		9 ft.

4 Name five items that would be best measured in centimeters or inches.

_____

_____

_____

_____

_____

REVIEW

 5 Use the ruler to measure the ribbons.

```
0 CM  1    2    3    4    5    6    7    8    9   10   11   12   13   14   15
```

a _____

b _____

c _____

d _____

 6 Use the ribbons above to complete the following.

a In the space above, draw a ribbon that is 12 cm long. Color it orange.

b What color ribbon is longest? _____

c What color ribbon is shortest? _____

d What colors are longer than the green ribbon? _____

e What color ribbon is shorter than the green ribbon? _____

f What is the difference in length between the shortest and longest ribbons? _____

g Write the colors of ribbons in order from longest (1) to shortest (5).

1 _____, 2 _____, 3 _____, 4 _____, 5 _____

7 Write the measurements marked on the ruler.

```
INCH    1        2        3        4        5        6
        a        b   c              d              e
```

a _____   **c** _____   **e** _____

b _____   **d** _____

© Shell Education

REVIEW

8 Measure these lengths in millimeters.

a _____ mm ——————————————————

b _____ mm ————————

c _____ mm ——————————————————————

d _____ mm —

e _____ mm ——————————

9 Find the perimeters.

a 6 cm / 1 cm (rectangle) P = _____ = _____

b 4 in. (square) P = _____ = _____

c 3 cm, 4 cm, 5 cm (triangle) P = _____ = _____

d 2 ft., 3 ft., 3 ft., 4 ft. (arrow) P = _____ = _____

e 4 m, 2 m (parallelogram) P = _____ = _____

f 2 in. (octagon) P = _____ = _____

ANGLES

An angle is the amount of turning between two straight line segments (arms) that meet at a point (vertex).

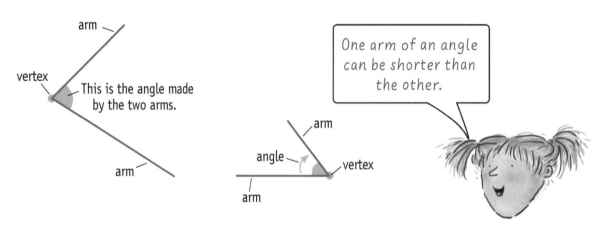

One arm of an angle can be shorter than the other.

Examples: Use red to trace the arms, color the angle blue, and draw a • on the vertex.

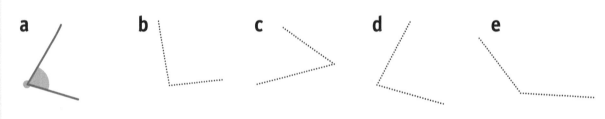

a   b   c   d   e

Your turn

Draw another arm in red to make each line into an angle. Color the angle blue, and draw a • on the vertex.

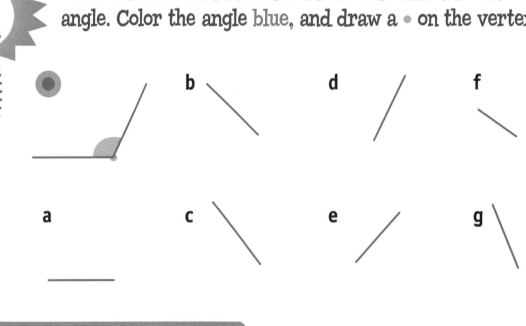

b   d   f

a   c   e   g

SELF CHECK   Mark how you feel

Got it!	Need help...	I don't get it

Check your answers
How many did you get correct?

PRACTICE

 1 Choose one angle in each picture. Use red to trace the arms of the angle. Then use blue to color the angle.

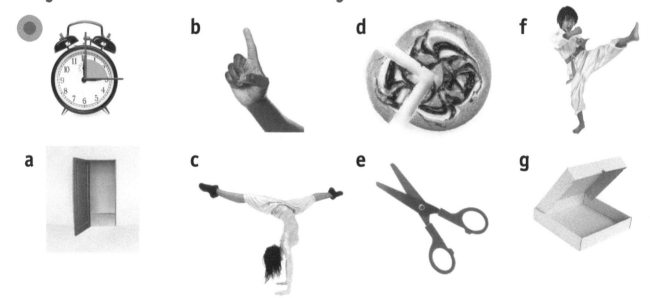

b   d   f

a   c   e   g

 2 Name and draw three objects around you that have angles.

a _____	b _____	c _____

 3 Use red to trace the angles you see in the picture. Draw a green dot on each vertex, and use blue to color the angle made.

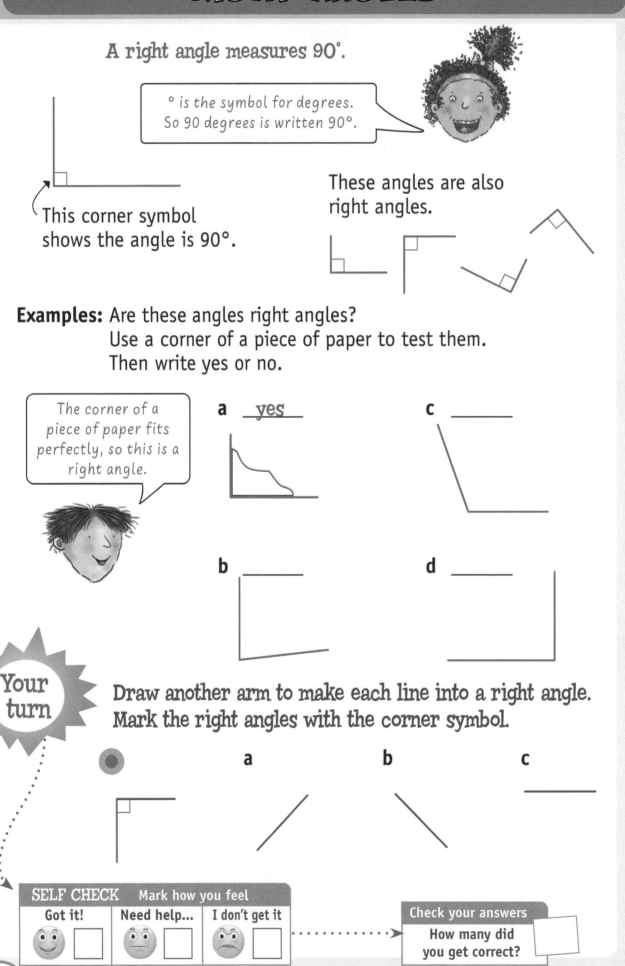

RIGHT ANGLES

A right angle measures 90°.

° is the symbol for degrees.
So 90 degrees is written 90°.

This corner symbol
shows the angle is 90°.

These angles are also
right angles.

Examples: Are these angles right angles?
Use a corner of a piece of paper to test them.
Then write yes or no.

The corner of a
piece of paper fits
perfectly, so this is a
right angle.

a <u>yes</u>

c _____

b _____

d _____

Your turn

Draw another arm to make each line into a right angle.
Mark the right angles with the corner symbol.

a   **b**   **c**

SELF CHECK   Mark how you feel

Got it!   Need help...   I don't get it

Check your answers
How many did
you get correct?

PRACTICE

1 Draw a checkmark on the right angles.

2 Draw four different right angles.

3 List five things that have right angles.

door

_____

_____

4 Label the angles as equal to (=), less than (<), or greater than (>) a right angle.

5 Use the corner symbol to mark the right angle in each shape.

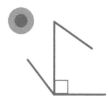   a    b    c

ACUTE AND OBTUSE ANGLES

Acute angles are less than 90°.

Obtuse angles are greater than 90°.

SCAN to watch video

< 90°   Narrow   Wide   > 90°

Example 1:
Draw another arm to make an acute angle. Color the angle blue.

a   b   c   d

Example 2:
Draw another arm to make an obtuse angle. Color the angle blue.

a   b   c   d

Your turn

Write Acute or Obtuse for each angle.

_____Obtuse_____   b _____   d _____

a _____   c _____   e _____

SELF CHECK   Mark how you feel
Got it!   Need help...   I don't get it

Check your answers
How many did you get correct?

PRACTICE

1 Draw three angles that match each description.

Acute Angles	Obtuse Angles

2 Order the angles from most narrow (1) to widest (5).

5   1   4   3   2

a

b

3 Use orange to trace the acute angles and green to trace the obtuse angles.

    b   d   f   h

a   c   e   g   i

4 List four things that have acute angles.

a pencil tip _____

5 Color the acute angles orange and the obtuse angles green.

   a   b   c   d

© Shell Education

ANGLES REVIEW

1 Use red to trace the arms, color the angle blue, and draw a ● on the vertex.

a   b  c   d

2 Draw another arm in red to make angles. Color the angle blue and write the type of angle you made.

a _____ b _____ c _____

_____

3 Choose one angle in the picture. Use red to trace the arms of the angle. Then use blue to color the angle.

a  b  c  d

4 Mark the right angles with the corner symbol.

a  b  c   d   e

5 Draw another arm to make each line into a right angle.

a  b   c  d

© Shell Education

6 Use the corner symbol to mark the right angle in each shape.

a   b   c   d

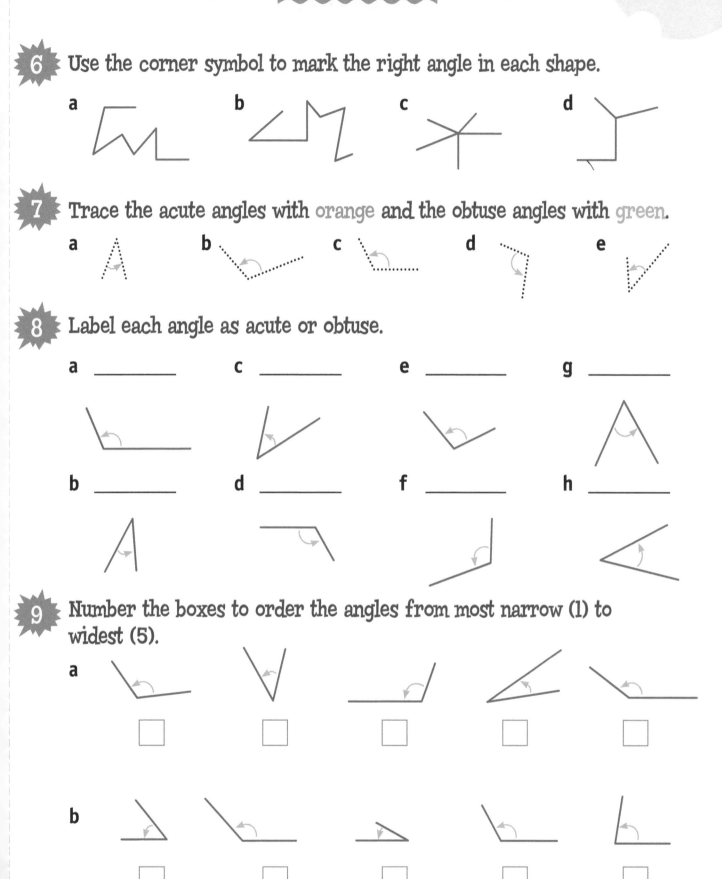

7 Trace the acute angles with orange and the obtuse angles with green.

a   b   c   d   e

8 Label each angle as acute or obtuse.

a _____   c _____   e _____   g _____

b _____   d _____   f _____   h _____

9 Number the boxes to order the angles from most narrow (1) to widest (5).

a

☐   ☐   ☐   ☐   ☐

b

☐   ☐   ☐   ☐   ☐

DIFFERENT TYPES OF LINES

Many shapes have lines that are vertical, horizontal, parallel, and perpendicular.

SCAN to watch video

Vertical lines go up and down.

Parallel lines never meet and are equal distances apart.

Horizontal lines go left to right.

Perpendicular lines meet at right angles.

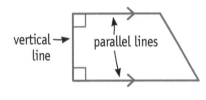

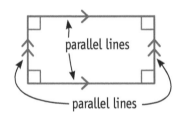

> It's easier to talk about shapes when you know the different types of lines.

Examples:

Trace the vertical lines with blue, horizontal lines with orange, parallel lines with green, and perpendicular lines with purple.

a   ——
c |
e ⊥
g ——
i |

b
d ⇐⇐
f ——
h ⊥
j //

Your turn

Draw three examples of each type of line.

Vertical	Horizontal	Parallel	Perpendicular
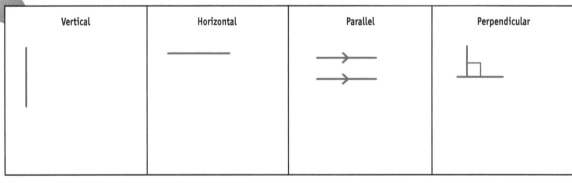			

SELF CHECK   Mark how you feel

Got it! ☐   Need help... ☐   I don't get it ☐

Check your answers
How many did you get correct?

© Shell Education

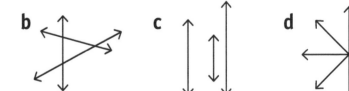 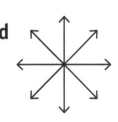

PRACTICE

1 Circle the lines that are parallel.

   a   **b**   **c**   **d**

2 Circle the lines that are perpendicular.

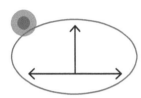   **a**   **b**   **c**   **d**

3 Circle the horizontal lines.

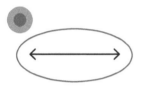   **a**   **b**   **c**   **d**

4 Circle the vertical lines.

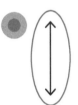   **a**   **b**   **c**   **d**

5 Trace the vertical lines with blue and horizontal lines with orange.

   **a**   **b**   **c**   **d**

6 List five things that have parallel lines.

   train tracks   **b** _____   **d** _____

a _____   **c** _____   **e** _____

TRIANGLES

Triangles are shapes that have 3 sides and 3 angles.
There are four different types of triangles.

SCAN to watch video

Equilateral
- All sides the same length
- All angles the same size
- Regular triangle

Isosceles
- Two sides the same length
- Two angles the same size
- Irregular triangle

Right
- One right angle
- Irregular triangle

Scalene
- All sides different lengths
- All angles different sizes
- Irregular triangle

> The marks on the sides and the angles tell you which ones are equal.

Examples: Put a check mark on the regular triangles and an *X* on the irregular triangles.

a ✗   b   c   d   e

Your turn

Trace the equilateral triangles in red, isosceles triangles in blue, scalene triangles in yellow, and right triangles in green.

   b   d   f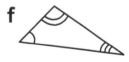

a   c   e   g

SELF CHECK   Mark how you feel

Got it!   Need help...   I don't get it

Check your answers
How many did you get correct?

© Shell Education

PRACTICE

1 Draw these shapes.

a Five different equilateral (regular) triangles

b Five different isosceles triangles

c Five different right triangles

d Five different scalene triangles

2 Match each label to the correct triangle.

All sides the same length

a Two angles the same size

b One right angle

Right triangle

Scalene triangle

Isosceles triangle

Equilateral triangle

c All sides different lengths

d Two sides the same length

e All angles different sizes

f All angles the same size

QUADRILATERALS

Quadrilaterals have four straight sides and four angles.

Squares are the only regular quadrilaterals.

All angles the same size.

All sides the same length.

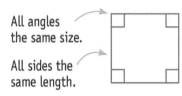

SCAN to watch video

Irregular quadrilaterals

Rectangle
- Opposite sides equal in length
- All angles 90°

Rhombus
- All sides equal in length
- Two pairs of parallel sides
- Opposite angles equal in size

Parallelogram
- Opposite sides equal in length
- Two pairs of parallel sides
- Opposite angles equal in size

Kite
- Two pairs of sides the same length
- No parallel sides

Trapezoid
- One pair of parallel sides

Examples:
Label each quadrilateral as regular or irregular.

a _____irregular_____

c _____

b _____

d _____

Your turn

Trace the squares in red, rectangles blue, parallelograms yellow, rhombuses green, trapezoids orange, and kites brown.

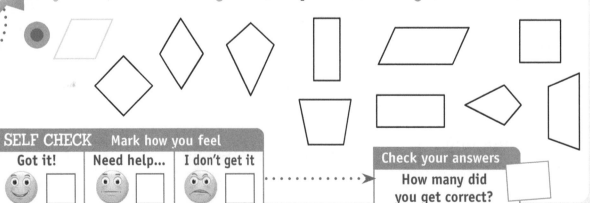

SELF CHECK   Mark how you feel

Got it!   Need help...   I don't get it

Check your answers

How many did you get correct?

© Shell Education

PRACTICE

1 Match each label to the correct shape.

	a	**b**
One pair of parallel sides	No parallel sides	Regular quadrilateral

 Square

 Rhombus

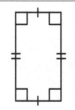 Rectangle

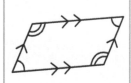 Parallelogram

 Trapezoid

 Kite

c	**d**	**e**	**f**
Two pairs of parallel sides and opposite angles equal in size	Opposite sides equal in length and all angles 90°	Opposite sides equal in length and opposite angles equal in size	All sides equal in length and opposite angles equal in size

2 Use purple to trace the parallel lines.

b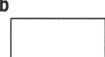

d

f

h

a

c

e

g

i

3 Use red to color the regular quadrilaterals and blue to color the irregular quadrilaterals.

b

d

f

h

a

c

e

g

i

© Shell Education

SYMMETRY

Symmetry is when one half of a shape is a mirror image, or reflection, of the other half.

This house is symmetrical because both halves fit on top of each other exactly.

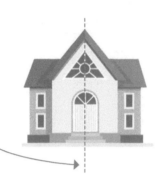

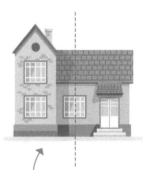

A line of symmetry is always dotted.

This house is not symmetrical because the two sides are not the same size.

Sometimes there is more than one line of symmetry.

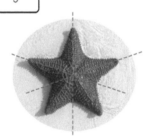

Examples: These shapes have one line of symmetry marked. Color half of each shape.

a   **b**   **c**   **d**

Your turn

1 Draw one line of symmetry through each shape. Then color half of the shape.

   a   **b**   **c**   **d**

2 Mark the shapes in Question 1 that have more than one line of symmetry.

SELF CHECK   Mark how you feel

Got it!	Need help...	I don't get it
☺ ☐	😐 ☐	☹ ☐

Check your answers
How many did you get correct?

© Shell Education

PRACTICE

1 Put a check mark next to the symmetrical shapes and an *X* next to the shapes that are not symmetrical.

 ✔   **b**    **d**   **f**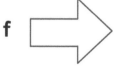

a   **c**    **e**    **g**

2 Use these shapes to answer the following questions.

   A   **B**   **C**   **D**   **E**   **F**   **G**   **H**

a Draw lines of symmetry on the symmetrical shapes above.

b Which shapes are symmetrical? _____

c Which shapes are not symmetrical? _____

d Which shapes have more than one line of symmetry? _____

3 Write your name in block letters.
Draw in any lines of symmetry on the letters.

4 Complete the pictures so that they are symmetrical.

    **a**    **b** 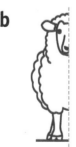   **c**

SHAPES REVIEW

 1 Fill in the table.

	Shape	Name	Number of angles	Number of sides	Number of corners
a					
b					
c					
d					
e					

 2 Draw an example of each type of line.

Vertical	Perpendicular	Parallel	Horizontal

3 Name the triangles.

a _____   c  _____

b _____   d  _____

  © Shell Education

4 Match each description to a type of triangle.

A regular shape

All angles different sizes

Two angles the same size

All sides the same length

Scalene triangle

Isosceles triangle

Right triangle

Equilateral triangle

All sides different lengths

One right angle

All angles the same size

Two sides the same length

5 Name the quadrilaterals.

a _____

b _____

c _____

d _____

e _____

f  _____

© Shell Education

REVIEW

 Match each label to the correct shape.

a

| Regular quadrilateral |

c

| No parallel sides |

e

| One pair of parallel sides |

  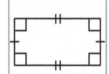 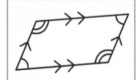 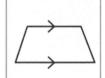

b

| Two pairs of parallel sides and opposite angles equal in size |

d

| Opposite sides equal in length and all angles 90° |

f

| Opposite sides equal in length and opposite angles equal in size |

g

| All sides equal in length and opposite angles equal in size |

 Circle the symmetrical shapes.

a   b   c   d   e   f

 Draw four symmetrical shapes.

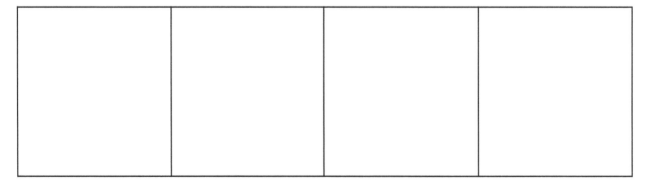

© Shell Education

9 Draw lines of symmetry on the shapes that are symmetrical.

a   b 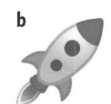 c  d  e

 10 Draw four shapes that have more than one line of symmetry.

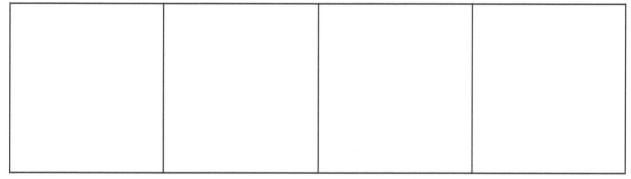

 11 Complete the pictures so that they are symmetrical.

a

b

c

d

AREA

Area is the size of a surface that an object covers.

Elise's Backyard

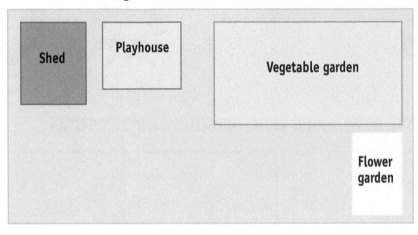

If a shape takes up more space than another shape, it has a larger area.

The area of the vegetable garden is the largest area because it covers the biggest amount of the surface of Elise's backyard.

The area of the flower garden is the smallest area because it covers the smallest amount of the surface of Elise's backyard.

Examples: Mark the shape with the larger area.

a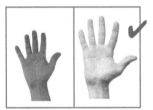

b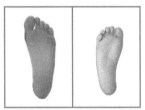

c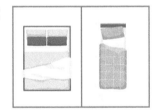

Your turn

Draw a similar shape with a larger area.

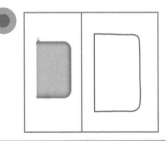

a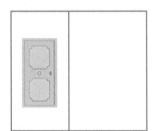

b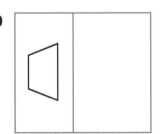

SELF CHECK Mark how you feel

Got it!	Need help...	I don't get it
☐	☐	☐

Check your answers
How many did you get correct?

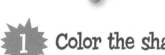

PRACTICE

1 Color the shape with the largest area blue and the shape with the smallest area green.

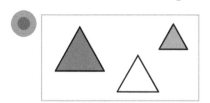   **a** 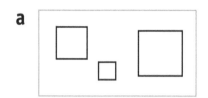   **b**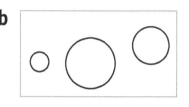

2 Circle the shape that has the smallest area.

   **b**    **d**

a    **c**   **e**

3 Color the shape that has the largest area.

     a   **b**

4 Order these shapes from smallest area (1) to largest area (5).

| 2 | 3 | 5 | 1 | 4 |

a

b

c

MEASURING AREA WITH UNITS

Areas can be measured with objects that are smaller than the area being measured

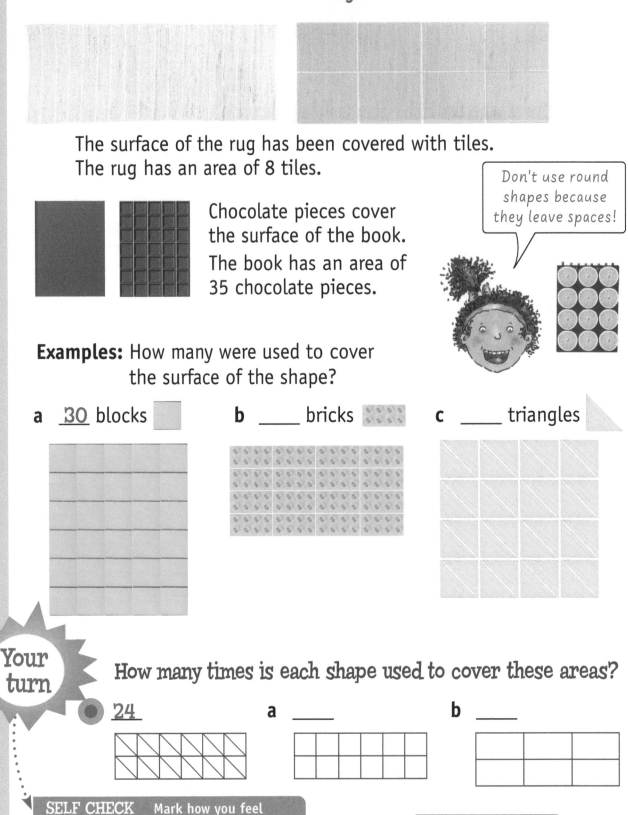

The surface of the rug has been covered with tiles.
The rug has an area of 8 tiles.

Chocolate pieces cover the surface of the book.
The book has an area of 35 chocolate pieces.

Don't use round shapes because they leave spaces!

Examples: How many were used to cover the surface of the shape?

a <u>30</u> blocks

b _____ bricks

c _____ triangles

Your turn

How many times is each shape used to cover these areas?

<u>24</u>

a _____

b _____

SELF CHECK Mark how you feel

Got it!

Need help...

I don't get it

Check your answers

How many did you get correct?

© Shell Education

PRACTICE

1 How many times is the square used to cover each area?

● <u>83</u>

a ___

b ___

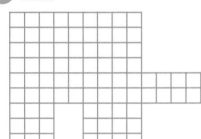
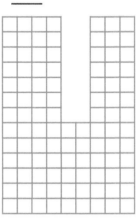
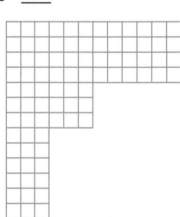

2 Len covered the surfaces of three books with sticky notes.

Purple book

Blue book

Green book

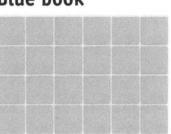

● The purple book has an area of _____32_____ sticky notes.

a The green book has an area of _____ sticky notes.

b The blue book has an area of _____ sticky notes.

c The _____ book has the largest area.

d The _____ book has the smallest area.

e The difference in area between the purple and blue books is _____ sticky notes.

f The difference in area between the blue and green books is _____ sticky notes.

g The difference between the book with the largest area and the book with the smallest area is _____ sticky notes.

h The total area of all three books is _____ sticky notes.

MEASURING AREAS USING A GRID

Grids can be used to measure area.
All the shapes in the grid must be the same shape and size.

A grid using squares

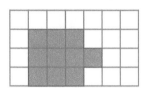

The red shape has an area of 10 squares.

A grid using rectangles

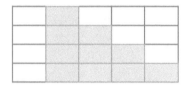

The blue shape has an area of 10 rectangles.

Examples:

a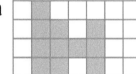

The orange shape has an area of _11_ squares.

b

The green shape has an area of _____ triangles.

 Your turn Write the area.

● _20_ rectangles

a ___ squares

b ___ triangles

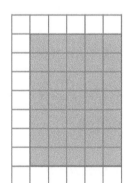

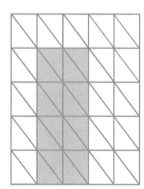

SELF CHECK   Mark how you feel

Got it!   Need help...   I don't get it

Check your answers

How many did you get correct?

PRACTICE

1 How many shapes has each surface been covered with?

● <u>25</u> rectangles   **a** __ squares   **b** __ squares   **c** __ triangles

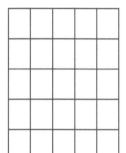 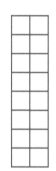 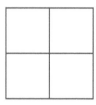 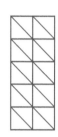

2 Using the grid paper, color a shape with each area.

● 12 squares   **a** 15 squares   **b** 20 squares   **c** 18 squares

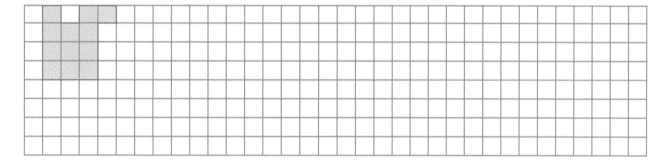

3 Find the area of each book cover by counting the number of squares used to cover the surface.

Jokes	20
Tall Tales	
China Today	
Tiny Tales	

4 Write the difference in area.

a *Jokes* and *China Today*   _____ squares

b *Tiny Tales* and *Tall Tales*   _____ squares

c *Tall Tales* and *Jokes*   _____ squares

d *Jokes* and *Tiny Tales*   _____ squares

SQUARE CENTIMETERS AND INCHES

Square centimeters (cm²) is a unit of measurement used to measure small areas. Square inches (sq. in.) can also be used to measure small areas.

SCAN to watch video

one square centimeter

1 cm
1 cm

one square inch

1 in.
1 in.

You can use multiplication to calculate the area of squares and rectangles— multiply the length by the width.

width

length

Area = length × width
= 2 cm × 4 cm
= 8 cm²

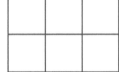

You can also count squares to calculate area.

Examples: Find the area.

a

Area = <u>length</u> × <u>width</u>

= <u>1 cm</u> × <u>4 cm</u>

= <u>4</u> cm²

b

Area = _____ × _____

= _____ × _____

= _____ in.²

Your turn

What is the area?

Area = <u>length</u> × <u>width</u>

= <u>1 in.</u> × <u>6 in.</u>

= <u>6</u> sq. in.

a

Area = _____ × _____

= _____ × _____

= _____ cm²

SELF CHECK   Mark how you feel

Got it!   Need help...   I don't get it

Check your answers

How many did you get correct?

© Shell Education

PRACTICE

Use the grid and shapes to answer the following questions.

							D					
A				C								
									E			
B												

 1 Complete the table.

	Shape	Area in words	Area using cm²
	A	six square centimeters	6 cm²
a	B		
b	C		
c	D		
d	E		

 2 Use the shapes above to fill in the gaps.

a Shape _____ has the largest area.

c Shape _____ has an area of 10 cm².

b Shape _____ has the smallest area.

3 Draw four different shapes that each have an area of 12 sq. in.

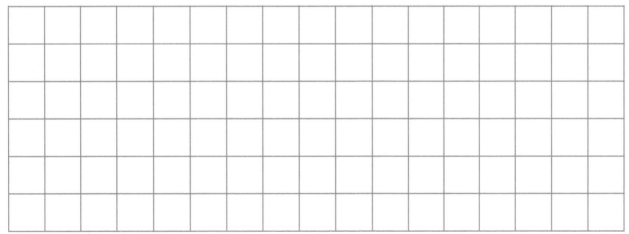

SQUARE METERS AND FEET

Larger areas are measured using square feet (ft.²) or square meters (m²).

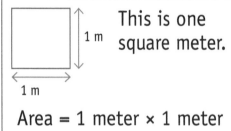

This is one square meter.

Area = 1 meter × 1 meter
= 1 m²

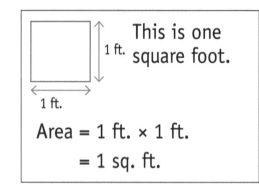

This is one square foot.

Area = 1 ft. × 1 ft.
= 1 sq. ft.

SCAN to watch video

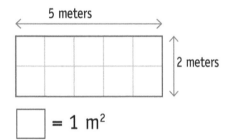

5 meters

2 meters

☐ = 1 m²

You would use square meters or feet to measure the board in your classroom.

The area of the board is 10 m².

Area = length × width
= 2 m × 5 m
= 10 m²

> What do you think is the area of the floor in your classroom?

Examples: Calculate the area.

a

4 ft.

2 ft.

Area = _____ × _____

= _____ × _____

= _____ ft.²

b

3 m

3 m

Area = _____ × _____

= _____ × _____

= _____ m²

Your turn

Circle the items that have an area of less than 1 sq. ft.

SELF CHECK Mark how you feel

Got it! ☐

Need help...   ☐

I don't get it ☐

Check your answers
How many did you get correct?

© Shell Education

PRACTICE

1 Draw each area on the grid.

○ 8 ft.²

a 6 ft.²

b 4 ft.²

c 10 ft.²

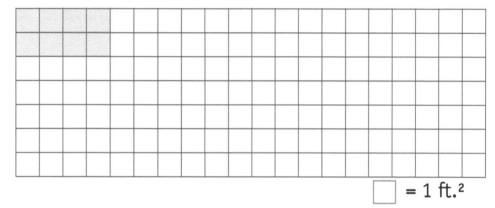

☐ = 1 ft.²

2 This is where Avdo lives.
How many square meters?

○ garden __5 m²__

a house _____

b shed _____

c pool _____

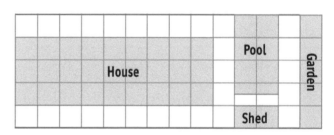

☐ = 1 m²

3 Complete the sentences.

● The largest area is the __house__.

a The smallest area is the _____.

b The _____ has an area of 7 m².

c The total area is _____.

d The difference in area between the pool and the garden is _____.

4 List four things larger than 1 ft.²

_____

5 List four things smaller than 1 m².

_____

SHAPES WITH THE SAME AREA

These shapes are different, but they all have an area of 10 cm².

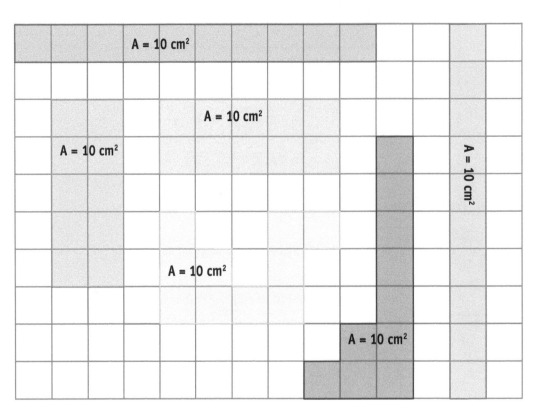

Examples: Finish the shapes so they have an area of 10 in.²

Draw three shapes with an area of 8 cm².

SELF CHECK   Mark how you feel

Got it!   Need help...   I don't get it

Check your answers

How many did
you get correct?

© Shell Education

PRACTICE

1 Draw as many rectangles as you can with an area of 24 cm².

☐ = 1 cm²

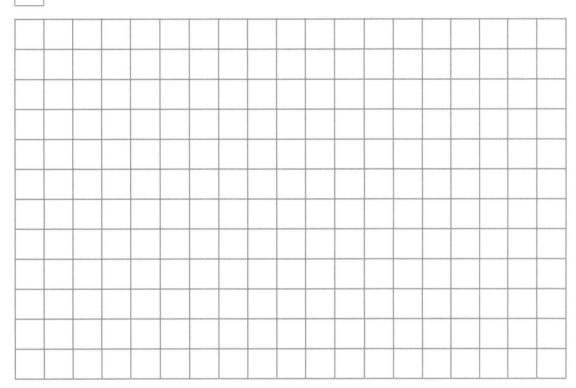

2 Color the shapes that have an area of 12 in.²   ☐ = 1 in.²

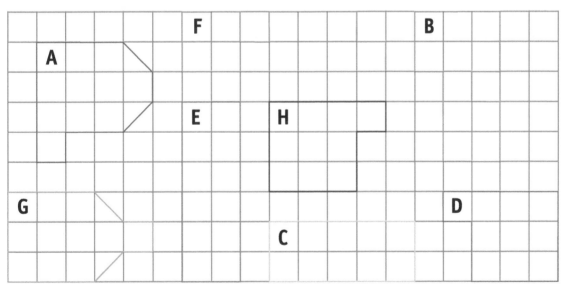

a Shapes _____ have an area of 12 sq. in.

b Shapes _____ do not have an area of 12 sq. in.

c Shape A has an area of _____.

d Shape D has an area of _____.

PERIMETER

The perimeter (P) is the distance around the outside of a shape. Add the lengths of all the sides to find the perimeter.

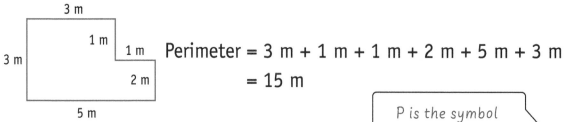

Perimeter = 3 m + 1 m + 1 m + 2 m + 5 m + 3 m

= 15 m

> P is the symbol used for perimeter.

Examples: Find the perimeter.

a

P = 2 in. + 4 in. + 2 in. + 4 in.

= <u>12</u> in.

b

P = 3 cm + 3 cm + 3 cm + 3cm

= _____ cm

Your turn

Find the perimeter.

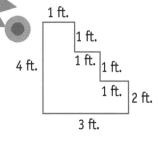

P = <u>1</u> ft. + <u>1</u> ft. + <u>1</u> ft. + <u>1</u> ft.

+ <u>1</u> ft. + <u>2</u> ft. + <u>3</u> ft. + <u>4</u> ft.

= <u>14</u> ft.

a

P = _____ cm + _____ cm + _____ cm +

_____ cm = _____ cm

b

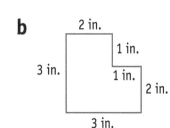

P = _____ in. + _____ in. + _____ in. +

_____ in. + _____ in. + _____ in.

= _____ in.

SELF CHECK   Mark how you feel

Got it!   Need help...   I don't get it

Check your answers

How many did you get correct?

PRACTICE

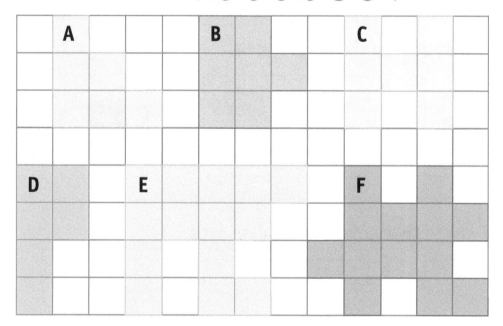

= 1 cm²

1 Find the perimeter of each shape.

A = <u>1 cm + 1 cm + 1 cm + 1 cm + 1 cm + 1 cm + 3 cm + 3 cm = 12 cm</u>

a B = _____

b C = _____

c D = _____

d E = _____

e F = _____

2 Write the missing letters.

a Shapes _____, _____, and _____ have the smallest perimeter.

b Shapes _____ and _____ have the largest perimeter.

3 Draw and label shapes with the given perimeters.

● 8 in.   **a** 12 in.   **b** 20 in.

1 in.

3 in.

© Shell Education

AREA REVIEW

 1 Mark the shape that covers the larger area.

a  **b** 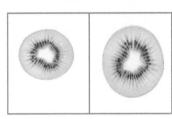 **c**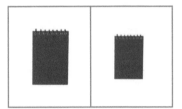

 2 Draw a similar shape that covers a smaller area.

a 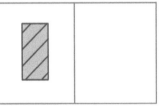 **b** 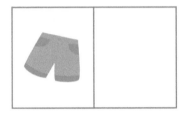 **c**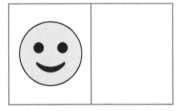

 **3** Color the shape with the largest area red and the shape with the smallest area blue.

a  **b**  **c**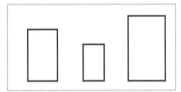

4 Number the shapes to order them from largest (1) to smallest (5) area.

a

b

c

© Shell Education

5 Write the missing numbers.

a _____ square blocks cover the surface of this shape.

b _____ bricks cover the surface of this shape.

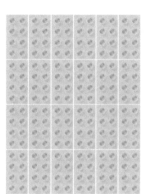

c _____ triangles cover the surface of this shape.

6 How many times is the square used to cover each shape?

a _____

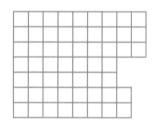

b _____

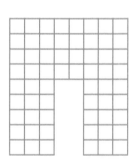

c _____

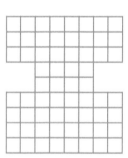

7 Write the missing numbers.

a

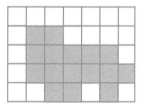

The orange shape has an area of _____ squares.

b

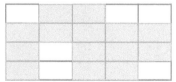

The blue shape has an area of _____ rectangles.

c

The purple shape has an area of _____ triangles.

REVIEW

 Calculate the area. □ = 1 cm²

a

Area = _____ × _____

= _____ × _____

= _____ cm²

b

Area = _____ × _____

= _____ × _____

= _____ cm²

c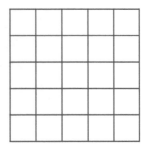

Area = _____ × _____

= _____ × _____

= _____ cm²

 What is the area of these rectangles? □ = 1 in.²

a

Area = _____ × _____

= _____ × _____

= _____ in.²

b

Area = _____ × _____

= _____ × _____

= _____ in.²

c

Area = _____ × _____

= _____ × _____

= _____ in.²

 © Shell Education

Match each shape to the correct area label. $\square$ = 1 cm²

a

A = 14 cm²

A = 10 cm²

A = 17 cm²

A = 7 cm²

A = 5 cm²

b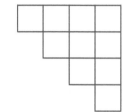

c

d

e

 Draw five different rectangles with an area of 14 in.² $\square$ = 1 in.²

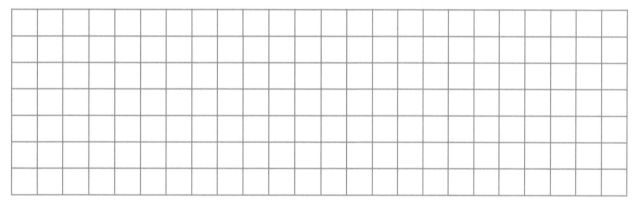

 Name four things that have an area:

a greater than 1 m²

_____

_____

b less than 1 in.²

_____

_____

REVIEW

 13 Write the area. ☐ = 1 m²

a _____

c _____

e _____

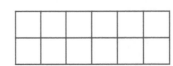

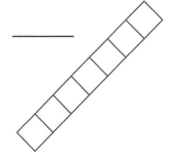

b _____

d _____

f _____

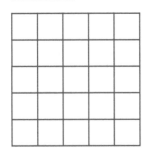

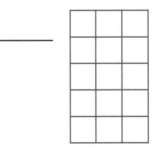

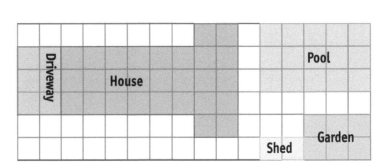

14 This is where Arlo lives. How many square feet?

a driveway _____

b house _____

c pool _____

d garden _____

e shed _____

f the total area of where Arlo lives _____

☐ = 1 ft.²

15 Write the place that has:

a the largest area. _____

b the smallest area. _____

 16 What is the difference in area?

a house and pool _____

c driveway and pool _____

b garden and shed _____

d shed and house _____

© Shell Education

17 Color the shapes that have an area of 10 m². ☐ = 1 m²

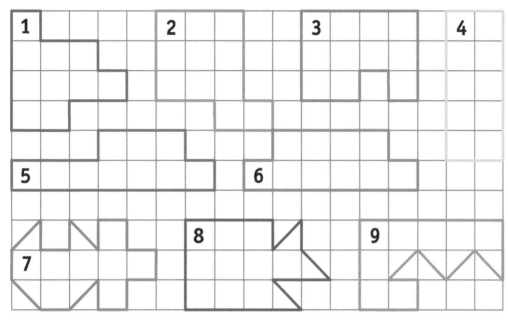

 18 Find the perimeter.

a
5 ft.
2 ft. [rectangle] 2 ft.
5 ft.

P = _____

= _____ ft.

b
1 cm
2 cm
4 cm
2 cm
2 cm
3 cm

P = _____

= _____ cm

c
6 m
2 m
3 m
1 m   5 m
1 m
2 m
3 m

P = _____

= _____ m

d
1 in.
2 in.
1 in.   5 in.
2 in.
2 in.
1 in.
4 in.

P = _____

= _____ in.

CAPACITY

Capacity is the amount of liquid a container can hold.

The green bucket has the largest capacity because it can hold the most liquid.

The yellow bucket has the smallest capacity because it can hold the least liquid.

Bottle A   Bottle B

Bottle A has more juice in it than Bottle B.

But Bottle B can hold more juice than Bottle A, so it has a larger capacity.

The larger container has the larger capacity.

Examples: Circle the container with the smaller capacity.

a

b

c

Your turn

Draw a similar object with a smaller capacity.

a

b

SELF CHECK   Mark how you feel

Got it!   Need help...   I don't get it

Check your answers

How many did you get correct?

© Shell Education

PRACTICE

 1 Number the containers to order them from smallest capacity (1) to largest capacity (5).

| 1 | 4 | 3 | 5 | 2 |

a

□ □ □ □ □

b

□ □ □ □ □

 2 Amir used each container to fill the yellow bucket. He tallied the number of times each one was filled.

	Medicine cup	Glass	Mug	Pot
Tally	┼┼┼┼ ┼┼┼┼ ┼┼┼┼ ┼┼┼┼	┼┼┼┼ ┼┼┼┼	┼┼┼┼ ‖	‖
Total	20	10	7	1

a How many times did Amir fill the pot to fill the yellow bucket? _____

b How many times did Amir fill these containers to fill the yellow bucket?

- medicine cup _____   • glass _____   • mug _____

c Which container has the least capacity? _____

d Which container has the most capacity? _____

LITERS AND GALLONS

Liters (L) and gallons (gal.) are used to measure how much space a liquid takes up.

1 liter = 1,000 milliliters

1 L = 1,000 mL

This container can measure one liter.

This container can measure one gallon.

Examples: How many liters or gallons can each container hold?

a ___1___ gal.   b _____ L   c _____ gal.   d _____ L

Your turn

Circle the containers that hold more than one gallon.

SELF CHECK   Mark how you feel

Got it!	Need help...	I don't get it

Check your answers

How many did you get correct?

PRACTICE

1 Circle the containers that hold less than one liter.

  a  b   c  d

e  f g   h  i

2 Think of three containers that would hold more than a gallon.
Draw them.

3 Nancy is buying drinks for a party. She needs 10 liters of cola,
7 liters of lemonade, and 3 liters of orange soda.
Color the 1-liter bottles Nancy needs to buy.

Cola	🍾 🍾 🍾 🍾 🍾 🍾 🍾 🍾 🍾 🍾
Lemonade	🍾 🍾 🍾 🍾 🍾 🍾 🍾 🍾 🍾 🍾
Orange soda	🍾 🍾 🍾 🍾 🍾 🍾 🍾 🍾 🍾 🍾

MEASURING LITERS AND GALLONS

The same amount of liquid can look different in different containers.

These containers each have two liters of juice in them.
Some containers look fuller than others because of their shape.

Examples: Color the containers to show 2 gallons.

Your turn

How much liquid is in each container?

 <u>2 L</u>

b _____

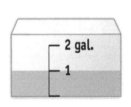

d _____

f _____

a _____

c _____

e _____

SELF CHECK   Mark how you feel

Got it!	Need help...	I don't get it

Check your answers

How many did you get correct?

PRACTICE

1 Color the number of 1-liter bottles needed to fill each bucket.

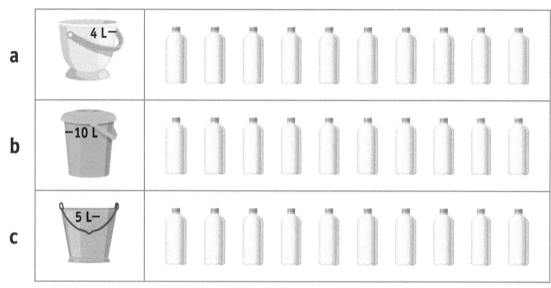

2 Color the pitchers to show the amounts.

● Pitcher A: 1 gal. **a** Pitcher B: 3 gal. **b** Pitcher C: 4 gal. **c** Pitcher D: 1 gal.

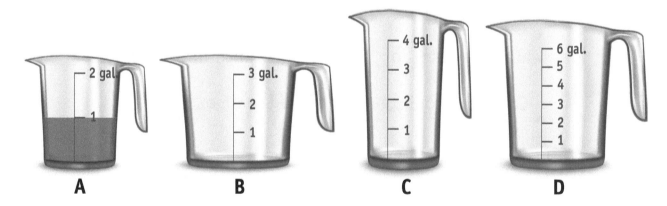

3 Use the pitchers above to answer the following questions.

a Which pitcher has the most liquid in it? _____

b Which pitcher has the least liquid in it? _____

c Write the capacity. Remember, capacity is how much a container is able to hold, not how much liquid is in the container.

Pitcher A	Pitcher B	Pitcher C	Pitcher D
2 gal.			

MILLILITERS, CUPS, AND FLUID OUNCES

We use milliliters (mL) to measure smaller amounts of liquid. There are 1,000 milliliters in one liter.
We can also measure small amounts of liquid in cups (c.) and fluid ounces (fl. oz.). There are 8 fluid ounces in 1 cup.

1,000 mL = 1 liter

750 mL = $\frac{3}{4}$ liter

500 mL = $\frac{1}{2}$ liter

250 mL = $\frac{1}{4}$ liter

1 c. = 8 fl. oz.

$\frac{3}{4}$ c. = 6 fl. oz.

$\frac{1}{2}$ c. = 4 fl. oz.

$\frac{1}{4}$ c. = 2 fl. oz.

Examples:

Mark the containers you would use milliliters or fluid ounces to measure.

a a cup of tea __X__

b water in a glass _____

c water in a bathtub _____

d water in a pool _____

e a dose of medicine _____

f juice in a juice box _____

Your turn

Color the containers to show the amounts.

● 1 L

b $\frac{1}{2}$ L

d $\frac{3}{4}$ L

a $\frac{1}{2}$ cup

c 1 cup

e $\frac{1}{4}$ cup

SELF CHECK   Mark how you feel

Got it!	Need help...	I don't get it

Check your answers

How many did you get correct?

PRACTICE

1 Write as liters.

- ● 1,000 mL ___1 L___

- **a** 250 mL _____

- **b** 750 mL _____

- **c** 500 mL _____

2 Write as milliliters.

- ● 2 L ___2,000 mL___

- **a** 3 L _____

- **b** $1\frac{1}{2}$ L _____

- **c** $2\frac{1}{4}$ L _____

3 Write as cups.

- ● 8 fl. oz. ___1 c.___

- **a** 6 fl. oz. _____

- **b** 2 fl. oz. _____

- **c** 4 fl. oz. _____

4 Write as fluid ounces.

- ● 3 c. ___24 fl. oz.___

- **a** 2 c._____

- **b** $2\frac{1}{2}$ c. _____

- **c** $1\frac{3}{4}$ c. _____

CAPACITY REVIEW

 1 Draw a similar container that has a smaller capacity.

a

b

c

 2 Hani used each container to fill a bin.
She tallied the number of times each one was filled.

	Tea cup	Glass	Beach bucket	Pot	Fish bowl
Tally	|||| |||| |||| |||| |||| |||| |||| |||| |||| |||| |||| |||| |||| |||| |||| ||||	|||| |||| |||| ||||	|||| |||	||||	||
Total	80	20	8	4	2

a How many times did Hani fill the containers to fill the bin?

- tea cup _____
- beach bucket _____
- fish bowl _____
- glass _____
- pot _____

b Which container has the smallest capacity? _____

c Which container has the largest capacity? _____

 3 Order the objects from largest capacity (1) to smallest capacity (5).

☐ ☐ ☐ ☐ ☐

© Shell Education

Draw three containers that hold more than 1 liter.

 Draw three containers that hold less than 1 gallon.

 What amount of liquid is in each container?

a _____ L   **b** _____ gal.   **c** _____ L

 Color each container to show the amounts.

a 2 gal.   **b** 4 L   **c** 5 gal.   **d** 3 L

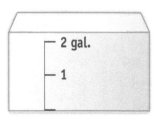   

8 How many milliliters?

a $\frac{1}{2}$ L _____

b 1 L _____

c $\frac{1}{4}$ L _____

d $\frac{3}{4}$ L _____

 9 How many fluid ounces?

a $\frac{3}{4}$ c. _____

b 1 c. _____

c $\frac{1}{4}$ c. _____

d $\frac{1}{2}$ c. _____

10 Color each pitcher to show the amount.

a 250 mL   c 750 mL   e 500 mL

b 4 fl. oz.   d 2 fl. oz.   f 8 fl. oz.

 11 Write as liters.

a 250 mL _____

b 1,000 mL _____

c 500 mL _____

d 250 mL _____

© Shell Education

12 Write as milliliters.

a $1\frac{1}{2}$ L _____ c $3\frac{1}{2}$ L _____

b $2\frac{1}{4}$ L _____ d $1\frac{3}{4}$ L _____

 13 Write as cups.

a 8 fl. oz. _____

b 2 fl. oz. _____

c 6 fl. oz. _____

d 4 fl. oz. _____

14 Write as fluid ounces.

a $2\frac{1}{2}$ c. _____ c $1\frac{1}{4}$ c. _____

b $1\frac{3}{4}$ c. _____ d $3\frac{1}{2}$ c. _____

KILOGRAMS AND POUNDS

Heavy items are measured in kilograms or pounds. The symbol for kilogram is kg. The symbol for pound is lb.

A carton of milk weighs about 1 kilogram (1 kg).

A shoe weighs about 1 pound (1 lb.).

Examples:

Circle the items that would be best measured in kilograms or pounds.

a 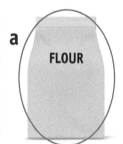 c  e  g   i

b  d  f  h   j

Your turn

Name six items that would be best measured in kilograms or pounds.

 _a bag of oranges_____   _____

_____   _____

_____   _____

SELF CHECK **SELF CHECK**   Mark how you feel

Got it!	Need help...	I don't get it
☐	☐	☐

Check your answers

How many did you get correct?

© Shell Education

PRACTICE

1 Color the weights to show the masses.

●	42 kilograms	10 kg	10 kg	10 kg	10 kg	10 kg	10 kg	10 kg	10 kg	10 kg	10 kg	
		5 kg	5 kg	5 kg	5 kg	5 kg	1 kg	1 kg	1 kg	1 kg	1 kg	
a	83 pounds	10 lbs.	10 lbs.	10 lbs.	10 lbs.	10 lbs.	10 lbs.	10 lbs.	10 lbs.	10 lbs.	10 lbs.	
		5 lbs.	5 lbs.	5 lbs.	5 lbs.	5 lbs.	1 lb.	1 lb.	1 lb.	1 lb.	1 lb.	
b	16 kilograms	10 kg	10 kg	10 kg	10 kg	10 kg	10 kg	10 kg	10 kg	10 kg	10 kg	
		5 kg	5 kg	5 kg	5 kg	5 kg	1 kg	1 kg	1 kg	1 kg	1 kg	
c	51 pounds	10 lbs.	10 lbs.	10 lbs.	10 lbs.	10 lbs.	10 lbs.	10 lbs.	10 lbs.	10 lbs.	10 lbs.	
		5 lbs.	5 lbs.	5 lbs.	5 lbs.	5 lbs.	1 lb.	1 lb.	1 lb.	1 lb.	1 lb.	

2 Write the mass that has been colored.

●	48 kg	10 kg	10 kg	10 kg	10 kg	10 kg	10 kg	10 kg	10 kg	10 kg	10 kg	
		5 kg	5 kg	5 kg	5 kg	5 kg	1 kg	1 kg	1 kg	1 kg	1 kg	
a	____ lbs.	10 lbs.	10 lbs.	10 lbs.	10 lbs.	10 lbs.	10 lbs.	10 lbs.	10 lbs.	10 lbs.	10 lbs.	
		5 lbs.	5 lbs.	5 lbs.	5 lbs.	5 lbs.	1 lb.	1 lb.	1 lb.	1 lb.	1 lb.	
b	____ kg	10 kg	10 kg	10 kg	10 kg	10 kg	10 kg	10 kg	10 kg	10 kg	10 kg	
		5 kg	5 kg	5 kg	5 kg	5 kg	1 kg	1 kg	1 kg	1 kg	1 kg	
c	____ lbs.	10 lbs.	10 lbs.	10 lbs.	10 lbs.	10 lbs.	10 lbs.	10 lbs.	10 lbs.	10 lbs.	10 lbs.	
		5 lbs.	5 lbs.	5 lbs.	5 lbs.	5 lbs.	1 lb.	1 lb.	1 lb.	1 lb.	1 lb.	

3 Write the masses in short form.

● 4 kilograms __4 kg__   c 17 kilograms _____

a twenty-three kilograms _____   d 1 pound _____

b ten pounds _____   e ninety-four kilograms _____

4 Put a check mark or an X on the masses to show if they are written correctly.

● ✔ 5 kg   b ☐ 2 kg   d ☐ 43 lbs.   f ☐ 100kG

a ☐ 14 KG   c ☐ 13 lB   e ☐ 17Kg   g ☐ 31 LBS.

5 Oliver's cardboard box can hold 8 kg.
How many of each item can he put into his box?

● __4__   a __   b __   c __   d __

| Grapes 2 kg | Bananas 1 kg | Raspberries 0.5 kg | Avocadoes 8 kg | Apples 4 kg |

6 Which items do you estimate have a mass of less than 1 kg? Mark them.

● ☑ an apple   d ☐ this book   h ☐ a sausage

a ☐ an orange   e ☐ a large dog   i ☐ an ice cream

b ☐ a television   f ☐ a horse   j ☐ a bag of chips

c ☐ a mobile phone   g ☐ a pair of   k ☐ a motorcycle
                        scissors

7 Use these items to complete the following questions.

| Watermelon 8 lbs. | Cantaloupe 4 lbs. | Coconuts 10 lbs. | Oranges 6 lbs. | Pineapple 2 lbs. |

a Which is the heaviest item? _____

b Which is the lightest item? _____

c How many pineapples weigh the same as one watermelon? _____

d Which two items together weigh 18 lbs.?

   _____ and _____

e How much do the oranges and the cantaloupe weigh together? _____

f List the items in order from lightest (1) to heaviest (5).

_____

    © Shell Education

8 How much would three of these items weigh?

● watermelon <u>24 kg</u>   **b** coconuts _____   **d** pineapple _____

a cantaloupe _____   **c** oranges _____

9 Circle the item that could be getting weighed

● **1 kg**

- a basketball
- (• a packet of flour)

b **5 kg**

- a watermelon
- an egg

d **2 kg**

- 2 L of milk
- a sandwich

a **6 lbs.**

- an apple
- a chicken

c **100 lbs.**

- a boy
- a watermelon

e **2 lbs.**

- a cup of tea
- a carton of milk

10 Name four things that match each description.

a Weigh less than one pound

_____

b Weigh about one pound

_____

c Weigh more than one pound

_____

11 Use the bags to answer the questions.

a Which bag weighs the most? _____

b Which bag weighs the least? _____

A: 32 kg   B: 15 kg   C: 5 kg

D: 40 kg   E: 53 kg

c What is the difference in weight?

- A and B _____   • C and D _____   • E and D _____

d How much do all the bags weigh altogether? _____

GRAMS AND OUNCES

A gram is a unit of measurement used to weigh light objects. There are 1,000 grams in one kilogram. An ounce is also used to weigh light objects. There are 16 ounces in a pound.

SCAN to watch video

The short form of gram is g.

A paperclip weighs about 1 gram (1 g).

The short form of ounces is oz.

An eraser weighs about 1 ounce (1 oz).

Examples:

Circle the objects that would be best measured in grams or ounces.

Your turn

Name six items that would be best measured in grams or ounces.

● a bag of chips _____   _____

_____   _____

_____   _____

SELF CHECK Mark how you feel

Got it!	Need help...	I don't get it
☺ ☐	😐 ☐	☹ ☐

Check your answers

How many did you get correct?

© Shell Education

PRACTICE

1 Use the short form to write these masses.

● three hundred grams <u>300 g</u>

a nine ounces _____

b fourteen ounces _____

c one hundred two grams

_____

d eighty ounces _____

e ninety-eight grams _____

f six thousand, one hundred fifteen grams

_____

2 Order the cans from smallest mass (1) to largest mass (8).

● [4]  PEAS 220 g

b [ ]  TOMATOES 525 g

d [ ]  CORN 490 g

f [ ] CHICKPEAS 935 g

a [ ] BEANS 120 g

c [ ]  TUNA 90 g

e [ ]  SOUP 410 g

g [ ] SPICE 25 g

3 Use the cans above to answer the questions.

a Which can has the largest mass? _____

b Which can has the smallest mass? _____

c Which cans have a mass less than 500 g? _____

d Which cans have a mass more than 500 g? _____

4 Circle the items that would be best measured in grams or ounces.

MASS REVIEW

 1 Write the missing words.

a Heavy items can be weighed in _____ or _____ .

b The symbol for kilogram is _____. The symbol for pound is _____.

 2 Circle the items that would be best measured in kilograms or pounds.

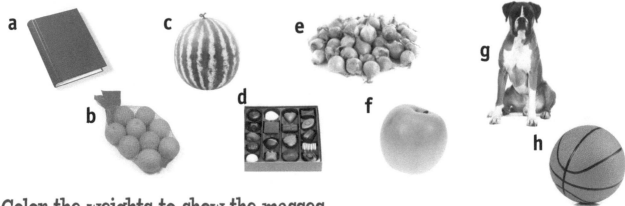

a c e g

b d f h

 3 Color the weights to show the masses.

a	32 pounds	10 lbs.	10 lbs.	10 lbs.	10 lbs.	10 lbs.	10 lbs.	10 lbs.	10 lbs.	10 lbs.	10 lbs.
		5 lbs.	5 lbs.	5 lbs.	5 lbs.	5 lbs.	1 lb.	1 lb.	1 lb.	1 lb.	1 lb.
b	18 kilograms	10 kg	10 kg	10 kg	10 kg	10 kg	10 kg	10 kg	10 kg	10 kg	10 kg
		5 kg	5 kg	5 kg	5 kg	5 kg	1 kg	1 kg	1 kg	1 kg	1 kg
c	41 pounds	10 lbs.	10 lbs.	10 lbs.	10 lbs.	10 lbs.	10 lbs.	10 lbs.	10 lbs.	10 lbs.	10 lbs.
		5 lbs.	5 lbs.	5 lbs.	5 lbs.	5 lbs.	1 lb.	1 lb.	1 lb.	1 lb.	1 lb.
d	52 kilograms	10 kg	10 kg	10 kg	10 kg	10 kg	10 kg	10 kg	10 kg	10 kg	10 kg
		5 kg	5 kg	5 kg	5 kg	5 kg	1 kg	1 kg	1 kg	1 kg	1 kg

 4 Write the mass that has been colored.

a		10 kg	10 kg	10 kg	10 kg	10 kg	10 kg	10 kg	10 kg	10 kg	10 kg
		5 kg	5 kg	5 kg	5 kg	5 kg	1 kg	1 kg	1 kg	1 kg	1 kg
b		10 lbs.	10 lbs.	10 lbs.	10 lbs.	10 lbs.	10 lbs.	10 lbs.	10 lbs.	10 lbs.	10 lbs.
		5 lbs.	5 lbs.	5 lbs.	5 lbs.	5 lbs.	1 lb.	1 lb.	1 lb.	1 lb.	1 lb.
c		10 kg	10 kg	10 kg	10 kg	10 kg	10 kg	10 kg	10 kg	10 kg	10 kg
		5 kg	5 kg	5 kg	5 kg	5 kg	1 kg	1 kg	1 kg	1 kg	1 kg

© Shell Education

REVIEW

5 Write the masses in short form.

a 6 kilograms _____

b twenty-nine pounds _____

c fifty kilograms _____

d 84 pounds _____

e 193 kilograms _____

f 205 pounds _____

g ninety-nine kilograms _____

h seventy-eight pounds _____

6 Put a check mark or an X on the masses to show if they are written correctly.

a ☐ 15 kg   c ☐ 305 KG   e ☐ 274 LBS.   g ☐ 81 kg

b ☐ 49 lBs   d ☐ 73 lbs.   f ☐ 9 kG   h ☐ 2 lbs.

7 Use the bags to answer the following questions.

A 12 lbs.   B 6 lbs.   C 18 lbs.   D 2 lbs.   E 10 lbs.

a Which bag is lightest? _____

b Which bag is heaviest? _____

c Which two bags together weigh 24 lbs.? _____ and _____

d How much do Bags A, D, and E weigh altogether? _____

e What is the difference in weight between Bag C and Bag E? _____

f How much would three of Bag A weigh? _____

g How much would four of Bag C weigh? _____

h Order the bags from heaviest to lightest.

☐ ☐ ☐ ☐ ☐

REVIEW

8 Circle the item that could be getting weighed.

a | 2 lbs. |
- a carton of milk
- an apple

c | 10 lbs. |
- a baby
- an orange

e | 180 lbs. |
- a young child
- an adult

b | 10 kg |
- a cup of water
- a small dog

d | 2 kg |
- a package of meat
- a sandwich

f | 1 kg |
- a wallet
- a pineapple

9 Name four things that match each description.

a weigh about one pound

_____

b weigh less than one pound

_____

c weigh more than one pound

_____

10 Circle the items that would be best measured in grams or ounces.

a pen

b magazine

c TV

d cotton candy

e suitcase

f toddler

g fish

h pepper

i handbag

j shoes

                    © Shell Education

11 Write in short form.

a seven hundred two grams _____

b ninety-nine ounces _____

c two thousand six hundred twenty grams _____

d fifteen ounces _____

e three hundred seventy-three grams _____

f eight ounces _____

g eighty grams _____

h one hundred six ounces _____

i six thousand three hundred four grams _____

j seven hundred twenty ounces _____

k three thousand six grams _____

 12 Use these cans to answer the following questions.

LENTILS 425 g

SALMON 90 g

TOMATOES 914 g

SOUP 510 g

PEAS 100 g

a Write the masses of the cans in order from lightest (1) to heaviest (5).

REVIEW

b The can of _____ has the largest mass and the can of _____ has the smallest mass.

c Which cans have a mass more than 500 g?

_____

d Which cans have a mass less than 500 g?

_____

e What is the difference in mass?

• tomatoes and peas _____

• lentils and salmon _____

• soup and salmon _____

• tomatoes and lentils _____

f How many more grams for each can do you need to make 1 kg?

• lentils _____

• salmon _____

• tomatoes _____

• soup _____

• peas _____

 © Shell Education

TIMETABLES

A timetable is a chart that tells you when something is due to happen. Timetables are also called schedules.

SCAN to watch video

Timetables can tell you when a train is due to arrive and leave, when your favorite TV show is on, or when recess starts.

Bayside Bus Timetable

Rose St.	7:33	8:07	3:06
Daisy Ave.	7:34	8:08	3:07
Forest Road	7:35	8:09	3:08
Tulip St.	7:38	8:12	3:11
Cherry Lane	7:43		3:16
Lotus Lane	7:47	8:21	3:20

Timetables are an important part of our lives, and they help keep us organized.

Examples: Use the bus timetable to answer the questions.

a The 7:33 bus has __5__ stops.

b The 8:07 bus has _____ stops.

c The earliest bus from Rose Street is at _____.

d The last stop on the 7:33 bus is _____.

Your turn

Answer these questions using the timetable above.

The __8:08__ bus from Daisy Avenue arrives at Tulip St at 8:12.

a The 8:07 bus does not stop at _____.

b It takes _____ minutes for the 3:06 bus to get from Forest Road to Lotus Lane.

c It takes _____ minutes for the 7:33 bus to get from Daisy Avenue to Tulip Street.

SELF CHECK   Mark how you feel
Got it! | Need help... | I don't get it

Check your answers
How many did you get correct?

PRACTICE

 1 Use the timetable to answer the following questions.

Jr. Lifeguard Camp Schedule			
Time	**Green Group**	**Blue Group**	**Red Group**
9:00–10:00 am	Flags	Beach Swim	CPR
10:00–11:15 am	CPR	Flags	Paddleboards
Recess			
11:40–12:45 pm	Paddleboards	CPR	Beach Swim
Lunch			
1:45–3:15 pm	Beach Swim	Paddleboards	Flags

● What group does flags 9:00–10:00 am? __green group__

a The _____ group does flags 1:45–3:15 pm.

b Which group does paddleboards at 10 am? _____

c The _____ group does beach swim at 1:45 pm.

d What time does red group start CPR? _____

e What time does camp finish? _____

f What time does recess start? _____

g What time does lunch finish? _____

h How long does the green group do paddleboards for? _____

i How long does the red group do flags for? _____

j How long does the blue group do flags for? _____

k How many activities does each group do? ___

l How many hours do the sessions before recess go for? _____

m How many hours does camp go for from start to finish? _____

   © Shell Education

2 Use the timetable to answer the questions.

● How long does it take for the buses to get to the pool from Best Street Elementary School?

_____15 minutes_____

a How long is the roll call?

_____

b How much time is scheduled to complete the breaststroke heats?

_____

c How long is recess?

_____

d How long is lunch?

_____

e How much longer are the heats than the finals?

_____

f How long does it take to complete all the finals for every event?

_____

g What time is cheerleading?

_____

h When is the teacher's race? _____

i What time does the field trip finish? _____

Best Street Elementary School Swim Field Trip	
8:45 am	Buses depart Best Street Elementary School
9:00 am	Roll call and Welcome
9:15 am	Freestyle heats
10:00 am	Backstroke heats
10:45 am	Breaststroke heats
11:30 am	Recess and Cheerleading
12:00 pm	Butterfly heats
12:45 pm	Freestyle finals
1:05 pm	Backstroke finals
1:25 pm	Breaststroke finals
1:45 pm	Lunch
2:35 pm	Teacher's Race and Carnival Point Count
2:45 pm	Buses depart for Best Street Primary School
3:00 pm	Presentations
3:15 pm	Return to Best Street Elementary School

Train Schedule					
Waterview	–	08:33	–	–	09:10
Lakeside	–	08:36	–	08:39	09:13
Pleasant Valley	–	08:41	–	08:44	09:18
Oakhill	–	08:50	–	08:53	09:27
Southland	08:49	08:54	09:00	08:57	09:31
Turtle Bay	08:51	08:56	09:04	–	09:33
East Creek	08:59	09:04	09:12	–	09:41
Temple	09:16	09:21	09:29	–	09:58
Mountainside	–	09:25	09:33	–	10:02
Lookout Point	09:27	09:31	09:39	–	10:08
Cliff's Edge	09:40	09:44	09:33	09:52	10:25

3 Use the train timetable above to answer the questions.

 What time does the 08:33 Waterview train arrive at Mountainside?

_9:25_

a When does the 08:39 am Lakeside train arrive at Southland? _____

b Someone boarding the 08:59 train from
East Creek would arrive at Cliff's Edge at _____.

c If someone boarded the 09:10 train from Waterview, would they say
"Good morning" or "Good afternoon" when they arrived at Cliff's Edge?

_____

4 When does the 09:10 train from Waterview arrive at these stops?

 Lakeside _9:13_   b Oakhill _____

a Turtle Bay _____   c Lookout Point _____

5 How long is the journey?

a Waterview to Lookout Point on the 08:33 Waterview train _____

b Southland to Temple on the 09:10 train from Waterview _____

c Turtle Bay to Mountainside on the 09:00 train from Southland

_____

                                                    © Shell Education

TIME REVIEW

1 Use the timetable to answer the following questions.

Fourth Grade Art Gallery Tour			
Class	**Room 10**	**Room 12**	**Room 14**
9:00–10:00 am	Drawing	Clay	Painting
10:00–11:00 am	Clay	Drawing	Collage
Recess			
11:30–12:30 pm	Painting	Collage	Drawing
Lunch			
1:30–2:30 pm	Collage	Painting	Clay

a Which class does clay from 10:00–11:00 am? _____

b Which class does painting first? _____

c Which class does collage last? _____

d How many activities does each class do? _____

e How long does recess go for? _____

f What time does lunch start? _____

g How many hours, including breaks, do the excursion activities go for?

_____

REVIEW

2 Use the train timetable to answer the questions.

Liverdale or Lisome to City via Frankstone						
Liverdale	4:02	–	4:32	5:02	–	5:32
Westview	4:07	–	–	–	–	5:37
Woodville	4:10	–	–	–	5:10	5:40
Vista	4:15	4:18	4:42	5:12	5:15	5:45
Morebel	4:19	4:21	–	–	5:18	5:49
Frankstone	4:24	4:26	–	–	5:23	5:54
Seecamp	4:31	4:33	–	–	5:30	6:01
Barrickville	4:39	4:41	–	–	5:38	6:09
Central	4:45	4:47	5:07	5:37	5:44	6:15
St Petars	4:54	4:56	5:16	5:46	5:43	6:24

a What time does the 4:02 Liverdale train arrive at Central? _____

b When does the 4:18 train from Vista arrive at Seecamp? _____

c If I have to be in St Petars by 5:30 pm,
what train should I catch from Liverdale? _____

d On the 5:32 Liverdale train, how long is the journey from:

- Westview to Morebel? _____
- Woodville to Seecamp? _____

- Central to St Petars? _____
- Liverdale to St Petars? _____

 3 How many stops are there?

a 4:18 train from Vista to St Petars _____

b 5:02 train from Liverdale to Central _____ _____

c 5:10 train from Woodville to Barrickville _____

© Shell Education

1. WHOLE NUMBERS

Three-Digit Numbers

Page 9 – Example(s)

Example 2: nine, forty

900
40
6

Number	H	T	O
946	9	4	6

Page 9 – Your Turn

	Number	Hundreds	Tens	Ones
a	127	1	2	7
b	249	2	4	9
c	863	8	6	3
d	524	5	2	4
e	780	7	8	0

Page 10 – Practice

1 a two hundred and ninety-three
   b four hundred and fifty-one
   c seven hundred and sixty-four
   d five hundred and three
   e eight hundred and fifty
   f three hundred

2

	Number	Hundreds	Tens	Ones
a	410	4	1	0
b	324	3	2	4
c	568	5	6	8
d	879	8	7	9
e	903	9	0	3

3 Circled green:
   359, 319, 362, 347, 300
   Circled blue:
   721, 924, 422, 923, 426
   Circled red:
   188, 218, 748, 838, 878

Place Value to 1,000

Page 11 – Example(s)

Example 2: 7, 6, 3

Page 11 – Your Turn

1 a ones   d ones
   b hundreds   e tens
   c tens

2   9⑶6   4⑴5   6⑺1   4⑺2   2⑴5

   ⑶24   ⑺16   9⑻9   5⑷3   5⑶7

Page 12 – Practice

1 a 213   c 960
   b 758   d 505

2 Circled: 257, 452, 553, 159, 56, 59, 757, 157, 556

3 Crossed out: 937, 982, 993, 957, 909, 973, 987, 921

4 a ones   e tens   i tens
   b tens   f ones   j ones
   c ones   g hundreds   k hundreds
   d hundreds   h ones

Value and Three-Digit Numbers

Page 13 – Example(s)

Example 2: 100, 30, 6
Example 3: 800, 50, 9

Page 13 – Your Turn

a (24)3   d (2)87   g (8)74   j (6)49   m (1)18
b (71)4   e (3)24   h (4)92   k (99)9   n (24)7
c (13)9   f (90)3   i (73)6   l (71)1

Page 14 – Practice

1 a 371   c 258   e 989
   b 623   d 184

2 2⑹   3⑵6   2⑷6   ⑹   1⑹   74⑹

3 ⑺8   8⑺2   ⑺9   7⑺7   1⑺5   4⑺4

4 8⑶2   8⑷9   8⑹3   8⑷7   8⑻8

5 a 40   d 40   g 400   j 400
   b 4   e 40   h 40   k 4
   c 400   f 40   i 400

Number Expanders and Three-Digit Numbers

Page 15 – Your Turn

a

1	hundreds	8	tens	4	ones

		1	8	tens	4	ones

			1	8	4	ones

Page 16 – Practice

1 a

2	hundreds	7	tens	6	ones

		2	7	tens	6	ones

			2	7	6	ones

b

6	hundreds	0	tens	5	ones

		6	0	tens	5	ones

			6	0	5	ones

2 a 326   b 504   c 906

3 a 34 tens, 2 ones   c 649 ones
   b 7 hundreds, 2 tens, 4 ones

ANSWERS

Expanded Three-Digit Numbers

Page 17 – Example(s)
Example 3: 1, 9, 8
Example 4: 300 + 40 + 6
3, 4, 6

Page 17 – Your Turn
a 265 = 200 + 60 + 5
    = 2 hundreds + 6 tens + 5 ones
b 638 = 600 + 30 + 8
    = 6 hundreds + 3 tens + 8 ones

Page 18 – Practice
1 a 727 = 700 + 20 + 7   d 582 = 500 + 80 + 2
   b 850 = 800 + 50   e 500 = 500
   c 607 = 600 + 7   f 495 = 400 + 90 + 5

2 a 400 + 10   d 200 + 6   g 500 + 60 + 4
   b 300 + 50 + 9   e 300
   c 800 + 30 + 2   f 700 + 80 + 3

3 a 190   d 252   g 143   j 376
   b 430   e 355   h 984   k 612
   c 741   f 802   i 487   l 538

Four-Digit Numbers

Page 19 – Example(s)
Example 2: two thousand eight hundred seventy-three

Number	Th	H	T	O
2,873	2	8	7	3

Page 19 – Your Turn

	Number	Th	H	T	O	Words
a	4,692	4	6	9	2	four thousand six hundred ninety-two
b	5,300	5	3	0	0	five thousand three hundred

Page 20 – Practice
1 a seven thousand two hundred nineteen
   b three thousand four hundred ninety
   c two thousand five
   d eight thousand nine hundred forty-three

2 a 3, 4, 1, 2   b 4, 2, 3, 1   c 3, 4, 1, 2
3 a 4, 3, 2, 1   b 3, 1, 4, 2   c 3, 1, 4, 2
4 a 4,922   b 8,003   c 7,469

Place Value and Four-Digit Numbers

Page 21 – Example(s)
Example 2: 4, 9, 3, 0   Example 3: 8, 9, 7, 2

Th	H	T	O
4	9	3	0

Th	H	T	O
8	9	7	2

Page 21 – Your Turn
3,921   4,374   5,500   9,746   9,525
2,125   5,251   6,303   1,809

Page 22 – Practice
1 a 1,882   c 6,030
   b 3,047   d 9,280

2

	Number	Th	H	T	O
a	3,269	3	2	6	9
b	9,038	9	0	3	8
c	4,730	4	7	3	0
d	5,476	5	4	7	6
e	6,924	6	9	2	4

3 4,372 4,362 6,153 1,956 6,666
   1,483 2,140 8,147 3,482 4,040
   3,206 2,736 3,884 4,711 1,134 3,381
   4,370 5,296 8,706 9,283 4,635
   1,782 8,132 4,975 4,125 3,776

Value and Four-Digit Numbers

Page 23 – Example(s)
Example 2: 3,000, 400, 70, 2
Example 3: 1, 1,000, 300, 90, 7, 7

Page 24 – Your Turn
1 8,432, 8,936

2 2,294   1,157   458   3,866   5,490
   8,745   8,894   6,128

Page 24 – Practice
1 Circled: 142, 640, 343
2 Circled: 524, 599, 507

3 a 400   f 40   k 400   p 400
   b 4   g 4   l 4   q 4,000
   c 40   h 400   m 4,000
   d 4,000 i 4,000 n 4
   e 4   j 40   o 40

4 a 1   f 20   k 900   p 5
   b 300   g 2,000 l 40   q 20
   c 9,000 h 0   m 8,000
   d 100   i 600   n 7
   e 3   j 3,000 o 700

Number Expanders and Four-Digit Numbers

Page 25 – Example(s)
Example 2:

| 6 | Th | 8 | H | 4 | T | 5 | 0 |

| 6 | 8 | H | 4 | T | 6 | 0 |

| 6 | 8 | 4 | T | 5 | 0 |

| 6 | 8 | 4 | 5 | 0 |

ANSWERS

Page 25 – Your Turn

a

7	4	0	6
	74	0	6
		740	6
			7406

Page 26 – Practice

1 a 1 Th, 0 H, 3 T, 6 O   d 2 Th, 2 H, 5 T, 1 O
  b 4 Th, 5 H, 3 T, 2 O   e 3 Th, 5 H, 4 T, 5 O
  c 1 Th, 5 H, 8 T, 5 O

2 a 8,532   b 2,468   c 7,564

Expanded Four-Digit Numbers

Page 27 – Example(s)

Example 2:

2,000 + 30 + 5

Page 27 – Your Turn

a

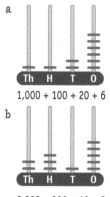

1,000 + 100 + 20 + 6

b

2,000 + 300 + 10 + 5

Page 28 – Practice

1 a 3,000 + 600 + 20 + 7   d 2,000 + 200 + 20 + 2
  b 4,000 + 800 + 3   e 7,000 + 600 + 40
  c 5,000 + 90 + 3

2 a 6,312   c 9,900   e 1,527
  b 7,025   d 4,203

3 a

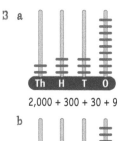

2,000 + 300 + 30 + 9

b

3,000 + 400 + 50 + 9

Ordering Four-Digit Numbers

Page 29 – Example(s)

Example 2: 9,283; 9,215; 6,258; 4,711; 3,724

Page 29 – Your Turn

1 a 3,788, 5,253, 8,873, 9,691   b 2,440, 6,440, 6,740, 9,894
2 a 7,791, 3,719, 2,020, 1,936   b 7,179, 2,904, 1,973, 1,503

Page 30 – Practice

1 a 1, 5, 2, 3, 4   c 5, 1, 4, 3, 2
  b 5, 4, 3, 2, 1   d 1, 5, 4, 2, 3
2 a 2, 5, 1, 4, 3   c 3, 1, 5, 4, 2
  b 2, 1, 3, 4, 5   d 1, 4, 5, 2, 3

Greater Than, Equal To, Less Than

Page 31 – Example(s)

Example 3: <
No
No
Yes

Page 31 – Your Turn

a True   c True   e False
b True   d False

Page 32 – Practice

1 a <   d >   g >
  b >   e >   h <
  c =   f <

2 a is greater than   d is less than   g is less than
  b is greater than   e is equal to   h is equal to
  c is greater than   f is greater than   i is greater than

3 a 19, 16, 18   e 127, 127, 127
  b 94, 95, 98   f 147, 214, 317, 234, 324
  c 41, 17, 9, 82, 73   g 607, 607, 607
  d 392, 497, 463

4 a >   d <   g <   j <
  b =   e <   h <   k <
  c >   f >   i >

5 Adult to check
6 Adult to check
7 Adult to check

8 a True   d True   g True
  b True   e False   h True
  c False   f True   i True

9 a 620, 262, 266, 594   e 5,231, 1,352, 1,325, 1,523
  b 714, 714, 714   f 9,729, 9,772
  c 224, 142, 242   g 3,439, 3,394
  d 928, 928, 928   h 8,352, 8,352, 8,352

10 a <   d <   g >
  b >   e <   h >
  c =   f >   i >

ANSWERS

Rounding to 100 and 1,000

Page 35 – Example(s)
Example 3: up, 9,000
Example 4: down, 21,000

Page 35 – Your Turn
1 a 700   b 2,400

2 a 10,000   b 24,000

Page 36 – Practice
1 a 1,700   c 1,000   e 2,600   g 4,900

  b 300   d 1,000   f 1,600   h 600

2 a 3,000   c 7,000   e 3,000

  b 5,000   d 6,000

3 a 4,900, 5,000   c 8,400, 8,000   e 6,500, 6,000

  b 3,100, 3,000   d 4,700, 5,000

Five-Digit Numbers

Page 37 – Example(s)
Example 3: thousand, hundred, twenty, five
Example 4: two, nine, fifty

Page 37 – Your Turn
1 24,957, 42,056, 73,950, 26,435, 17,537

2 a seventy-three thousand four hundred twenty

  b nineteen thousand five hundred ninety-six

  c eighty-four thousand two hundred fifty-three

Page 38 – Practice
1 a forty-nine thousand three hundred fifty

  b fifty-seven thousand four hundred twenty

  c sixty-two thousand nine hundred forty-three

  d eighty-one thousand four hundred sixty-two

  e ninety-three thousand two hundred fifty-eight

  f sixteen thousand four hundred twenty-two

2 a 53,847 fifty-three thousand eight hundred forty-seven

  b 71,329 seventy-one thousand three hundred twenty-nine

  c 94,382 ninety-four thousand three hundred eighty-two

  d 81,432 eighty-one thousand four hundred thirty-two

  e 76,218 seventy-six thousand two hundred eighteen

  f 62,471 sixty-two thousand four hundred seventy-one

  g 31,240 thirty-one thousand two hundred forty

Place Value to 100,000

Page 39 – Example(s)
Example 2: 4, 7, hundreds, ones

TT	Th	H	T	O
4	7	5	6	8

Page 39 – Your Turn
⑦③,⑥⓪⑧   ⑧⑨,②④③   ⑥③,⑧②⑤   ⑦④,①⓪③
⑥①,⓪⓪⓪   ④⑦,⓪⑨⓪   ③②,③⑥①   ②④,①④⓪

Page 40 – Practice
1 a 20,431   b 94,736   c 35,655   d 65,218

2

	Number	TT	Th	H	T	O
a	67,138	6	7	1	3	8
b	15,840	1	5	8	4	0
c	71,459	7	1	4	5	9
d	25,043	2	5	0	4	3
e	75,458	7	5	4	5	8

3

	TT	Th	H	T	O
a		5,000			
b					2
c			10		
d	80,000				
e					5
f				80	

The Value of Numbers to 100,000

Page 41 – Example(s)
Example 3: (from left to right) 20,000; 4,000; 700; 60; 9

Page 41 – Your Turn
②8,49①   ①0,39⑧   ②4,93⑦   8②,35⑧
⑨0,00⑨   ①2,68③   ⑦3,46⑨   ④4,44④
③5,29③   ④7,24⑦   ⑥4,29③

Page 42 – Practice
1 Adult to check

2 a 2,487   b 87   c 0   d 7

3 a 30,000   f 8   k 1,000   p 40,000

  b 10   g 90,000   l 600   q 4,000

  c 40,000   h 70   m 20   r 50

  d 2,000   i 400   n 80,000   s 7,000

  e 0   j 3   o 0

Greater Than, Equal To, Less Than: Numbers to 100,000

Page 43 – Example(s)
Example 3: >
Yes
No
No

Page 43 – Your Turn
  a No   b Yes   c Yes

Page 44 – Practice
1 a <   d <   g <   j <   m =

  b =   e >   h <   k =

  c <   f <   i >   l <

2 a is less than   c is less than

  b is greater than   d is equal to

3 Adult to check

Rounding to 10,000

Page 45 – Example(s)

Example 3: up, 20,000
Example 4: up, 90,000

Page 45 – Your Turn

a up, 40,000   b down, 50,000   c up, 80,000

Page 46 – Practice

1 a 40,000   c 60,000   e 80,000   g 90,000
   b 70,000   d 90,000   f 80,000   h 50,000

2 a 37,500, 37,500, 38,000, 40,000
   b 71,540, 71,500, 72,000, 70,000
   c 84,970, 85,000, 85,000, 80,000
   d 26,610, 26,600, 27,000, 30,000
   e 30,430, 30,400, 30,000, 30,000

Whole Numbers Review Page 47

1 a six hundred seventy-five
   b four hundred twenty-nine
   c three thousand fifty-six
   d two thousand three hundred fifty
   e seven thousand four hundred thirty-eight
   f eight thousand five hundred three
   g twenty-six thousand five hundred ninety
   h thirty-seven thousand four hundred twenty-nine

2

	Number	TT	Th	H	T	O
a	79	0	0	0	7	9
b	838	0	0	8	3	8
c	903	0	0	9	0	3
d	1,430	0	1	4	3	0
e	2,574	0	2	5	7	4
f	3,827	0	3	8	2	7
g	12,507	1	2	5	0	7
h	35,639	3	5	6	3	9
i	40,256	4	0	2	5	6
j	57,007	5	7	0	0	7

3 Circled: 836, 842, 3,863, 2,862, 19,837, 5,815, 29,836

4 Circled: 24,293, 4,684, 4,004, 94,362, 4,937, 34,876

5 a hundreds   f ten thousands   k ones
   b hundreds   g thousands   l ones
   c thousands   h hundreds   m tens
   d thousands   i thousands   n hundreds
   e ten thousands   j hundreds   o tens

6 a 60,304   e 80,063
   b 28,031   f 53,002
   c 478   g 40,068
   d 5,070   h 70,590

7 a 20   g 2   m 2
   b 2   h 20,000   n 200
   c 20   i 2,000   o 2,000
   d 2   j 200   p 20,000
   e 2,000   k 2,000   q 2,000
   f 200   l 20,000   r 200

8

2	thousands	7	hundreds	5	tens	9	ones

3	2	4	8	ones

4	ten thousands	6	thousands	8	hundreds	1	tens	9	ones

1	thousands	0	hundreds	3	tens	7	ones

9 a 600 + 30 + 2   d 1,000 + 400 + 30 + 8
   b 200 + 7   e 3,000 + 500 + 80 + 9
   c 900 + 10   f 7,000 + 100 + 30 + 6

10 a 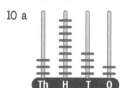   c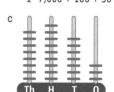

    b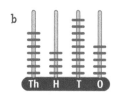

11 a >   d <   g <   j <
    b >   e >   h >   k >
    c =   f >   i =   l <

12

	Number	Nearest 10	Nearest 100	Nearest 1,000	Nearest 10,000
a	13,427	13,430	13,400	13,000	10,000
b	49,238	49,240	49,200	50,000	50,000
c	56,502	56,500	56,500	57,000	60,000
d	60,348	60,350	60,300	60,000	60,000
e	99,037	99,040	99,000	99,000	100,000
f	74,295	74,300	74,300	74,000	70,000
g	86,697	86,700	86,700	87,000	90,000

ANSWERS

2. ADDITION

Addition without Regrouping

Page 51 – Example(s)
Example 3: 97
Example 4: 97

Page 51 – Your Turn
a 92   b 88   c 83   d 97   e 98

Page 52 – Practice
1 a 39   c 89   e 87   g 79
   b 57   d 86   f 98

2 a 86   e 77   i 47   m 97   q 79
   b 79   f 88   j 88   n 86   r 99
   c 79   g 95   k 88   o 95   s 95
   d 96   h 79   l 52   p 67

3 a 52   c 45   e 20   g 20
   b 31   d 23   f 27

4 a 60 + 10, 70   g 40 + 30, 70
   b 80 + 20, 100   h 60 + 30, 90
   c 80 + 20, 100   i 40 + 40, 80
   d 70 + 20, 90   j 40 + 20, 60
   e 50 + 20, 70   k 50 + 60, 110
   f 70 + 20, 90

5 a 978   d 987   g 559
   b 979   e 979   h 988
   c 68   f 694

6 a 280   c 231   e 572
   b 233   d 121

7 a 260 + 20; 280   c 590 + 10; 600
   b 740 + 20; 760

Addition with Regrouping

Page 55 – Example(s)
Example 3: 91
Example 4: 112

Page 55 – Your Turn
a 173   b 91   c 110

Page 56 – Practice
1 a 114   c 86   e 61   g 141
   b 123   d 91   f 143

2 a 70   e 140   i 138   m 100   q 182
   b 120   f 143   j 111   n 74   r 82
   c 127   g 117   k 132   o 103   s 84
   d 133   h 146   l 84   p 123

3 a 34   e 38   i 25   m 57   q 58
   b 47   f 45   j 59   n 93   r 55
   c 54   g 67   k 13   o 65   s 36
   d 49   h 86   l 15   p 46

4 a 761   d 851   g 945   j 980
   b 990   e 696   h 482   k 901
   c 426   f 981   i 572

5 a 209   d 218   g 769   j 109   m 106
   b 135   e 219   h 369   k 186   n 367
   c 218   f 548   i 298   l 528

Addition Review Page 59

1 a 99   d 99   g 858
   b 94   e 759   h 999
   c 99   f 898   i 897

2 a 107   c 141   e 780
   b 161   d 490   f 1,070

3 a 24   d 32   g 527
   b 36   e 262   h 438
   c 45   f 315   i 149

4 a 60, 30, 90   d 30, 80, 110   g 540, 30, 570
   b 90, 40, 130   e 370, 80, 450   h 590, 20, 610
   c 40, 40, 80   f 650, 20, 670   i 750, 50, 800

3. SUBTRACTION

Subtraction without Regrouping

Page 61 – Example(s)
Example 4: 32
Example 5: 31
Example 6: 33

Page 61 – Your Turn
a 27   b 22   c 23

Page 62 – Practice
1 a 32   c 21   e 32   g 11
   b 16   d 22   f 19

2 a 35   c 34   e 33   g 51
   b 23   d 13   f 22

3 b Incorrect   f Correct
   c Incorrect   g Correct
   d Correct   h Incorrect
   e Correct   Mario got 5 out of 8.

Subtraction without Regrouping and Three-Digit Numbers

Page 63 – Example(s)
Example 4: 941   Example 5: 393   Example 6: 610

Page 63 – Your Turn
  a 415   b 856

Page 64 – Practice
1 a 402   d 921   g 100   j 181
   b 400   e 612   h 701   k 144
   c 134   f 116   i 401

2 a 416   c 845   e 511   g 463
   b 521   d 16   f 0

Subtraction with Regrouping and Two-Digit Numbers

Page 65 – Example(s)
Example 3: 38
Example 4: 29

Page 65 – Your Turn
  a 19   b 18   c 45

Page 66 – Practice
1 a 6   d 19   g 55   j 33
   b 6   e 38   h 9   k 29
   c 19   f 19   i 18

2 a 38, 38 + 33 = 71   d 16, 16 + 25 = 41
   b 39, 39 + 43 = 82   e 26, 26 + 34 = 60
   c 29, 29 + 64 = 93

Subtraction with Regrouping and Three-Digit Numbers

Page 67 – Example(s)
Example 3: 428
Example 4: 569

Page 67 – Your Turn
  a 297   b 286

Page 68 – Practice
1 a 416   d 684   g 688   j 507
   b 391   e 263   h 287   k 679
   c 219   f 486   i 171

2 a 418, 418 + 206 = 624   d 488, 488 + 356 = 844
   b 477, 477 + 235 = 712   e 286, 286 + 123 = 409
   c 488, 488 + 425 = 913

Subtraction with Regrouping and Four-Digit Numbers

Page 69 – Example(s)
Example 3: 6,785
Example 4: 3,203

Page 69 – Your Turn
1 a 2,507   b 1,564   c 527

Page 70 – Practice
1 a 5,749   c 9,366   e 888
   b 4,457   d 1,477

2 a 7,083   c 9,188   e 1,928
   b 842   d 7,457

3 a X (4,349)   b Check mark

Estimating Subtraction Answers

Page 71 – Example(s)
Example 2 (left to right): 1,000; 100; 900

Page 71 – Your Turn
1 a 610, 420, 190
2 a 500, 200, 300

Page 72 – Practice
1 a 1,350, 380, 970   e 29,390, 26,420, 2,970
   b 5,950, 3,270, 2,680   f 540, 170, 370
   c 700, 390, 310   g 63,530, 62,350, 1,180
   d 3,270, 2,130, 1,140

2 a 7,400, 4,200, 3,200   e 24,400, 19,400, 5,000
   b 51,800, 34,600, 17,200   f 900, 200, 700
   c 600, 300, 300   g 4,400, 2,500, 1,900
   d 4,400, 1,200, 3,200   h 6,100, 6,000, 100

Subtraction Review Page 74

1 a 32   d 52   g 14   j 311
   b 62   e 37   h 17   k 289
   c 62   f 19   i 111   l 589

2 a 2,465   c 2,322   e 4,779
   b 5,481   d 6,218   f 6,611

3 a 26, 26 + 32 = 58   c 424, 424 + 123 = 547
   b 49, 49 + 25 = 74   d 361: 361 + 253 = 614

4 a 4,214: 4,214 + 143 = 4,357
   b 6,429: 6,429 + 2,305 = 8,734

5 a wrong (39)   e wrong (650)
   b correct   f wrong (3,781
   c wrong (109)   g correct
   d correct   Score: 3 out of 7

6 a 530, 140, 390   c 3,520, 2,990, 530
   b 320, 210, 110   d 7,440, 4,320, 3,120

7 a 600, 200, 400   e 24,400, 15,700, 8,700
   b 500, 300, 200   f 53,300, 45,300, 8,000
   c 1,800, 400, 1,400   g 54,300, 51,800, 2,500
   d 2,900, 300, 2,600   h 73,200, 41,300, 31,900

4. MULTIPLICATION

Groups and Rows

Page 78 – Example(s)
Example 3: 1, 1, 6
Example 4: 6, 6, 5

Page 78 – Your Turn
1 a 5 b 6

2 a 2 b 3

Page 79 – Practice
1 a 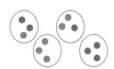 d

b 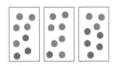 e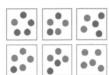

c

2 a

b

c

3 a 3 rows of 5 d 2 groups of 3 g 3 rows of 5
   b 4 rows of 6 e 3 groups of 4 h 2 rows of 9
   c 4 rows of 1 f 4 groups of 6

Repeated Addition to Solve Multiplication

Page 80 – Example(s)
Example 3: 20, 20, 20
Example 4: 6, 30, 6, 30

Page 80 – Your Turn
1 a 3 groups of 4 = 12   c 1 group of 4 = 4
     4 + 4 + 4 = 12   4 = 4
     3 × 4 = 12   1 × 4 = 4

   b 3 rows of 4 = 12
     4 + 4 + 4 = 12
     3 × 4 = 12

Page 81 – Practice
1 a
     5
     1 + 1 + 1 + 1 + 1 = 5
     5 × 1 = 5

   b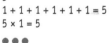
     9
     3 + 3 + 3 = 9
     3 × 3 = 9

   c
     16
     2 + 2 + 2 + 2 + 2 + 2 + 2 +
     2 = 16
     8 × 2 = 16

2 a 6 × 2 = 12   e 5 × 4 = 20   i 5 × 7 = 35
   b 4 × 2 = 8   f 5 × 5 = 25   j 6 × 6 = 36
   c 3 × 9 = 27   g 4 × 10 = 40
   d 5 × 1 = 5   h 7 × 4 = 28

Commutative Property

Page 82 – Example(s)
Example 3: 8, 5
Example 4: 12, 3 × 4 = 12

Page 82 – Your Turn
1 a   d

b  e

c

Page 83 – Practice
1 a 3 × 9   f 9 × 8   k 8 × 3   p 8 + 8
   b 5 + 4   g 10 × 9   l 3 + 9 + 1   q 4 × 9
   c 1 × 7   h 11 × 1   m 2 + 4 + 7   r 9 × 5
   d 2 + 8   i 6 × 2   n 4 × 3   s 7 × 6
   e 3 + 9   j 4 + 6   o 1 × 5

2 a  d

   Both equal 28.   Both equal 9.

   b 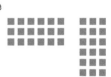 e

   Both equal 5.

                          Both equal 18.

   c

   Both equal 27.

© Shell Education

Inverse Operations of Multiplication and Division

Page 84 – Example(s)
Example 3: 5
Example 4: 60, 10

Page 84 – Your Turn
a 4, 4   c 4, 4   e 3, 3
b 4, 4   d 4, 4

Page 85 – Practice
1 a $25 \div 5 = 5$ d $36 \div 6 = 6$ g $24 \div 8 = 3$
   b $21 \div 3 = 7$ e $9 \div 1 = 9$
   c $40 \div 4 = 10$ f $48 \div 4 = 12$

2

a	$6 \times 2 = 12$	$12 \div 2 = 6$	$2 \times 6 = 12$	$12 \div 6 = 2$
b	$2 \times 5 = 10$	$10 \div 5 = 2$	$5 \times 2 = 10$	$10 \div 2 = 5$
c	$8 \times 5 = 40$	$40 \div 5 = 8$	$5 \times 8 = 40$	$40 \div 8 = 5$
d	$1 \times 7 = 7$	$7 \div 7 = 1$	$7 \times 1 = 7$	$7 \div 1 = 7$
e	$2 \times 12 = 24$	$24 \div 12 = 2$	$12 \times 2 = 24$	$24 \div 2 = 12$
f	$4 \times 5 = 20$	$20 \div 5 = 4$	$5 \times 4 = 20$	$20 \div 4 = 5$
g	$7 \times 4 = 28$	$28 \div 4 = 7$	$4 \times 7 = 28$	$28 \div 7 = 4$
h	$8 \times 4 = 32$	$32 \div 4 = 8$	$4 \times 8 = 32$	$32 \div 8 = 4$
i	$3 \times 11 = 33$	$33 \div 11 = 3$	$11 \times 3 = 33$	$33 \div 3 = 11$
j	$6 \times 7 = 42$	$42 \div 7 = 6$	$7 \times 6 = 42$	$42 \div 6 = 7$
k	$9 \times 10 = 90$	$90 \div 10 = 9$	$10 \times 9 = 90$	$90 \div 9 = 10$
l	$2 \times 9 = 18$	$18 \div 2 = 9$	$9 \times 2 = 18$	$18 \div 9 = 2$

Factors and Multiples

Page 86 – Example(s)
Example 3: 2, 4

Page 86 – Your Turn
a F   c T   e T
b T   d F

Page 87 – Practice
1 a 1, 2, 3, 4, 6, 8, 12, 24   d 1, 2, 3, 6, 9, 18
   b 1, 2, 5, 10   e 1, 5
   c 1, 2, 4, 5, 10, 20

2 a 4, 8, 12, 16, 20   d 5, 10, 15, 20, 25
   b 7, 14, 21, 28, 35   e 10, 20, 30, 40, 50
   c 6, 12, 18, 24, 30

3 a 5   d 9   g 5   j 8
   b 6   e 7   h 9   k 7
   c 9   f 4   i 8

4 a 14, 35, 49, 56, 21, 63   c 9, 81, 90, 108, 54, 72
   b 18, 30, 54, 48, 42, 24

Multiplying Two-Digit by Single-Digit Numbers

Page 88 – Example(s)
Example 2:
Using known facts: 8
$8 + 8 + 8 + 8 + 8$
120
Multiplying the tens and then the ones: 8, 8
40
120
15×8

	10	5
8	80	40

40
120

Page 88 – Your Turn
a $40 \times 7 = 280$ $= 4 \text{ tens} \times 7 + 7 \text{ twos}$
   $280 + 7 + 7$ $= 280 + 14$
   $= 294$ $= 294$

	40	2
7	280	14

$= 280 + 14$
$= 294$

Page 89 – Practice
1 a 52×5 e 88×8
   $50 \times 5 = 250$ $80 \times 8 = 640$
   $50 + 5 + 5$ $640 + 8 + 8 + 8 + 8 + 8 + 8 +$
   $= 260$ $8 + 8$
                    $= 704$
   b 19×6
   $10 \times 6 = 60$ f 34×7
   $60 + 6 + 6 + 6 + 6 + 6 +$ $30 \times 7 = 210$
   $6 + 6 + 6$ $210 + 7 + 7 + 7 + 7$
   $= 114$ $= 238$

   c 28×3 g 45×8
   $20 \times 3 = 60$ $40 \times 8 = 320$
   $60 + 3 + 3 + 3 + 3 + 3 +$ $320 + 8 + 8 + 8 + 8 + 8$
   $3 + 3$ $= 360$
   $= 84$

   d 97×4
   $90 \times 4 = 360$
   $360 + 4 + 4 + 4 + 4 + 4 + 4 + 4$
   $= 388$

2 a 58×4 d 71×8
   $= 4 \times 5 \text{ tens} + 4 \text{ eights}$ $= 8 \times 7 \text{ tens} + 8 \text{ ones}$
   $= 200 + 32$ $= 560 + 8$
   $= 232$ $= 568$

   b 463×3 e 62×5
   $= 3 \times 4 \text{ tens} + 3 \text{ sixes}$ $= 5 \times 6 \text{ tens} + 5 \text{ twos}$
   $= 120 + 18$ $= 300 + 10$
   $= 138$ $= 310$

   c 39×7
   $= 7 \times 3 \text{ tens} + 7 \text{ nines}$
   $= 210 + 63$
   $= 273$

3 a 63 × 7

	60	3
7	420	21

= 420 + 21
= 441

b 92 × 6

	90	2
6	540	12

= 540 + 12
= 552

c 32 × 8

	30	2
8	240	16

= 240 + 16
= 256

d 19 × 4 = 76

	10	9
4	40	36

= 40 + 36
= 76

e 86 × 3

	80	6
3	240	18

= 240 + 18
= 258

Multiplication Review Page 91

1 a 4, 3   b 5, 2   c 3, 4

2 a 6 rows of 2
2 + 2 + 2 + 2 + 2 + 2 = 12
2 × 6 = 12

b 4 groups of 2
2 + 2 + 2 + 2 = 8
2 × 4 = 8

c 3 rows of 5
5 + 5 + 5 = 15
3 × 5 = 15

d 6 groups of 3
3 + 3 + 3 + 3 + 3 + 3 = 18
3 × 6 = 18

3 a 4 × 8 = 32   c 4 × 6 = 24   e 4 × 1 = 4
   b 5 × 5 = 25   d 6 × 2 = 12   f 6 × 9 = 54

4 a 9 × 5   c 4 + 3 + 2   e 8 × 6
   b 4 × 7   d 2 + 5   f 8 + 7 + 5

5 a 36, 36, 4   d 7, 7   g 4, 32
   b 3, 3   e 7, 7   h 11, 11
   c 30, 30, 5   f 10, 10

6 a 1, 2, 3, 4, 6, 12   c 1, 2, 3, 4, 6, 9, 12, 18, 36
   b 1, 2, 4, 5, 10, 20   d 1, 2, 4, 5, 8, 10, 20, 40

7 a T   c T   e F   g T
   b T   d F   f T   h F

8 a 9, 18, 27, 36, 45   d 2, 4, 6, 8, 10
   b 3, 6, 9, 12, 15   e 1, 2, 3, 4, 5
   c 10, 20, 30, 40, 50   f 5, 10, 15, 20, 25

9 a

×	1	6	3	8	11	4
5	5	30	15	40	55	20
4	4	24	12	32	44	16
7	7	42	21	56	77	28
2	2	12	6	16	22	8
9	9	54	27	72	99	36

b

×	5	2	12	10	0	7
8	40	16	96	80	0	56
3	15	6	36	30	0	21
10	50	20	120	100	0	70
1	5	2	12	10	0	7
6	30	12	72	60	0	42

10 a 16 × 3
= 10 × 3 = 30
= 30 + 3 + 3 + 3 + 3 + 3 + 3
= 48
16 × 3
= 3 × 1 tens + 3 sixes
= 30 + 18
= 48
16 × 3

	10	6
3	30	18

= 30 + 18
= 48

b 42 × 6
= 40 × 6 = 240
= 240 + 6 + 6
= 252
42 × 6
= 6 × 4 tens + 2 sixes
= 240 + 12
= 252
42 × 6

	40	2
6	240	12

= 240 + 12
= 252

5. DIVISION

Grouping

Page 95 – Example(s)
Example 2: 16, 4, 4

Page 95 – Your Turn
a 2   b 3

Page 96 – Practice
1 a 3, 4   b 2, 6   c 4, 2   d 3, 6

2 a 5, 5   b 4, 4

3 a 36, 6   b 14, 2

Equal Rows

Page 97 – Example(s)
Example 3: 3, 5

Page 97 – Your Turn
a   b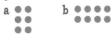

Page 98 – Practice
1 a 5, 5   c 2, 2   e 3, 3
   b 12, 12   d 1, 1

2 a 4 rows of 3   c 8 rows of 5
   b 3 rows of 4   d 2 rows of 9

Repeated Subtraction to Solve Division

Page 99 – Example(s)
Example 3: 18
18, 15
15, 12
12, 9
9, 6
6, 3
3, 0
6
6 times

Page 99 – Your Turn

a $9 \div 3 = 3$
Start at 9
$9 - 3 = 6$
$6 - 3 = 3$
$3 - 3 = 0$
3

b $14 \div 7 = 2$
Start at 14
$14 - 7 = 7$
$7 - 7 = 0$
2

c $12 \div 4 = 3$
Start at 12
$12 - 4 = 8$
$8 - 4 = 4$
$4 - 4 = 0$
3

Page 100 – Practice

1 a $45 \div 5 = 9$
$45 - 5 = 40$
$40 - 5 = 35$
$35 - 5 = 30$
$30 - 5 = 25$
$25 - 5 = 20$
$20 - 5 = 15$
$15 - 5 = 10$
$10 - 5 = 5$
$5 - 5 = 0$
9

b $24 \div 8 = 3$
$24 - 8 = 16$
$16 - 8 = 8$
$8 - 8 = 0$
3

c $30 \div 6 = 5$
$30 - 6 = 24$
$24 - 6 = 18$
$18 - 6 = 12$
$12 - 6 = 6$
$6 - 6 = 0$
5

d $35 \div 7 = 5$
$35 - 7 = 28$
$28 - 7 = 21$
$21 - 7 = 14$
$14 - 7 = 7$
$7 - 7 = 0$
5

e $12 \div 2 = 6$
$12 - 2 = 10$
$10 - 2 = 8$
$8 - 2 = 6$
$6 - 2 = 4$
$4 - 2 = 2$
$2 - 2 = 0$
6

Standard Algorithm

Page 101 – Example(s)

Example 3: Quotient: 3
3, 24

Page 101 – Your Turn

a 6, 6   b 6, 6   c 9, 9   d 12, 12

Page 102 – Practice

1 a 4   d 10   g 7   j 7
b 11   e 9   h 8   k 6
c 8   f 9   i 5

2 a 28, 28   c 6, 6   e 5, 5   g 60, 60
b 8, 8   d 5, 5   f 22, 22

3 a False   d False   g False   j True
b True   e False   h True   k False
c True   f True   i False

Division with Remainders

Page 103 – Example(s)

Example 2: 13, 2
6, 1
1
$13 \div 2 = 6$ remainder 1

Page 103 – Your Turn

a 2, 2
$12 \div 5 = 2$ remainder 2

Page 104 – Practice

1 a $15 \div 2 = 7$ remainder 1
b $18 \div 4 = 4$ remainder 2
c $48 \div 8 = 6$ remainder 0
d $25 \div 3 = 8$ remainder 1

e $21 \div 7 = 3$ remainder 0
f $29 \div 4 = 7$ remainder 1
g $83 \div 9 = 9$ remainder 2

2 a 4 r 2   c 4 r 3   e 9 r 2   g 12 r 2
b 9 r 2   d 5 r 2   f 10 r 1

3 a remainder 3   d remainder 4
b remainder 2   e remainder 5
c remainder 1

Division Review Page 105

1 a 2, 5   b 3, 4   c 4, 3

2 a 5, 5   b 6, 6   c 7, 7

3 a

5 rows of 4 = 20
$20 \div 5 = 4$

c

4 rows of 8 = 32
$32 \div 4 = 8$

b

3 rows of 4 = 12
$12 \div 3 = 4$

4 a

b

c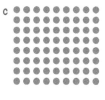

5 a $32 \div 4 = 8$
$32 - 4 = 28$
$28 - 4 = 24$
$24 - 4 = 20$
$20 - 4 = 16$
$16 - 4 = 12$
$12 - 4 = 8$
$8 - 4 = 4$
$4 - 4 = 0$

b $48 \div 12 = 4$
$48 - 12 = 36$
$36 - 12 = 24$
$24 - 12 = 12$
$12 - 12 = 0$

c $24 \div 6 = 4$
$24 - 6 = 18$
$18 - 6 = 12$
$12 - 6 = 6$
$6 - 6 = 0$

d $6 \div 6 = 1$
$6 - 6 = 0$

6 a 3×10 d 5×8 g 8×8 j 12×3
b 8×9 e 4×6 h 5×4
c 10×8 f 7×3 i 6×2

7 a 12   c 18   e 28   g 50   i 96
b 8   d 27   f 77   h 6   j 14

© Shell Education

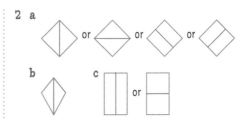

8 a 6   d 8   g 11   j 6
   b 3   e 9   h 12
   c 8   f 10   i 9

9 a 12   c 8   e 8
   b 4   d 7   f 12

10 a 4, 4   d 40, 40   g 8, 8   j 6, 6
   b 5, 5   e 7, 7   h 3, 3
   c 7, 7   f 12, 12   i 99, 99

11 a $23 \div 4 = 5 \text{ r } 3$ f $28 \div 9 = 3 \text{ r } 1$
   b $37 \div 12 = 3 \text{ r } 1$ g $63 \div 6 = 10 \text{ r } 3$
   c $43 \div 5 = 8 \text{ r } 3$ h $48 \div 10 = 4 \text{ r } 8$
   d $92 \div 10 = 9 \text{ r } 2$ i $25 \div 5 = 5 \text{ r } 0$
   e $14 \div 7 = 2 \text{ r } 0$ j $59 \div 12 = 4 \text{ r } 11$

12 a 5 r 3   c 7 r 3   e 5 r 2
   b 5 r 3   d 8 r 6   f 11 r 1

6. FRACTIONS

Numerators and Denominators

Page 110 – Example(s)

Example 4: $\frac{1}{4}$ Example 5: $\frac{3}{10}$ Example 6: one

Page 110 – Your Turn

Color all the top numbers red, color all the horizontal lines green, and color all the bottom numbers blue.

Page 111 – Practice

1 a 3   c 7   e 4   g 3
   b 1   d 2   f 4

2 a 8   c 5   e 2   g 5
   b 4   d 8   f 4

3 a three-eighths   d three-fifths   g one-eighth
   b one-fifth   e three-quarters   h five-eighths
   c seven-eighths   f two-quarters   i one-third

4 a $\frac{3}{4}$ b $\frac{4}{5}$ c $\frac{3}{8}$ d $\frac{3}{5}$ e $\frac{3}{3}$

5 a three-quarters   c three-eighths   e three-fifths
   b four-fifths   d three-fifths

Fractions—Halves

Page 112 – Example(s)

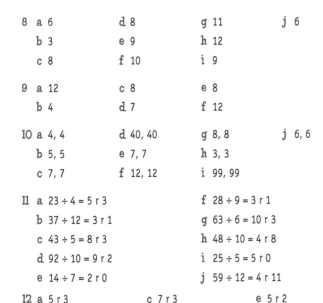

Example 3:   Example 4:

Circle: d, e, f, g

Page 113 – Practice

1 Checkmark: a, f, g

---

2 a

   b   c

3 Cross out b, f, h, j

Fractions—Quarters and Eighths

Page 114 – Example(s)

Example 2:   Example 4:

Page 114 – Your Turn

Color blue (quarters): g   Color red (eighths): a, c, e   Cross out: b, d, f

Page 115 – Practice

1

	Fraction name	Fraction	Picture
a	seven-eighths	$\frac{7}{8}$	
b	three-quarters	$\frac{3}{4}$	
c	five-eighths	$\frac{5}{8}$	
d	two-quarters	$\frac{2}{4}$	
e	six-eighths	$\frac{6}{8}$	
f	four-quarters	$\frac{4}{4}$	

2 (Sample answers provided; other answers are possible. All parts must be equal in size.)

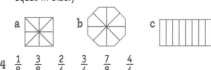

a   b   c

3 (Sample answers provided; other answers are possible. All parts must be equal in size.)

a   b   c

4 $\frac{1}{8}$ $\frac{3}{8}$ $\frac{2}{4}$ $\frac{3}{4}$ $\frac{7}{8}$ $\frac{4}{4}$

Fractions—Thirds and Fifths

Page 116 – Example(s)

Example 2:   Example 4:

Page 116 – Your Turn

Color purple (thirds): b, f, g   Color green (fifths): a, e   Cross out: c, d

© Shell Education

Page 117 – Practice

1

	Fraction name	Fraction	Picture
a	two-fifths	$\frac{2}{5}$	
b	two-thirds	$\frac{2}{3}$	
c	three-thirds	$\frac{3}{3}$	
d	four-fifths	$\frac{4}{5}$	
e	five-fifths	$\frac{5}{5}$	

2 $\frac{1}{5}$ $\frac{1}{3}$ $\frac{3}{5}$ $\frac{2}{3}$ $\frac{4}{5}$ $\frac{3}{3}$

3 a $\frac{2}{5}$ d $\frac{3}{3}$

   b $\frac{4}{5}$ e $\frac{1}{3}$

   c $\frac{5}{5}$

Simplifying Fractions

Page 118 – Example(s)

Example 4: $\frac{6}{10} = \frac{3}{5}$

divided by 2

Page 118 – Your Turn

   a 5   b 3   c $\frac{2}{7}$

Page 119 – Practice

1 a 3, 24, $\frac{1}{8}$ c 4, 40, $\frac{1}{10}$

   b 5, 20, $\frac{1}{4}$

2 a ÷5, $\frac{3}{4}$ c ÷50, $\frac{1}{2}$ e ÷6, $\frac{3}{5}$ g ÷5, $\frac{8}{9}$

   b ÷3, $\frac{3}{4}$ d ÷7, $\frac{3}{4}$ f ÷8, $\frac{3}{5}$

Comparing Fractions

Page 120 – Example(s)

Example 4: one-eighth $\frac{1}{8}$ or one-tenth $\frac{1}{10}$

Page 120 – Your Turn

   a 4, 4   b 3, 3   c 5, 5

Page 121 – Practice

1 a 3, 2, 5, 4, 6, 1   b 5, 6, 4, 2, 1, 3

2 a =   d >   g >   j >

   b >   e <   h =   k =

   c <   f <   i =

3 Adult to check

4 Adult to check

5 Adult to check

Equivalent Fractions

Page 122 – Example(s)

Example 3: 5, 2

Page 122 – Your Turn

   a 2   b 2   c 1

Page 123 – Practice

1 a $\frac{3}{4}$ is equivalent to $\frac{6}{8}$

   b $\frac{1}{2}$ is equivalent to $\frac{2}{4}$

   c $\frac{6}{10}$ is equivalent to $\frac{3}{5}$

   d $\frac{4}{8}$ is equivalent to $\frac{2}{4}$

   e $\frac{1}{4}$ is equivalent to $\frac{2}{8}$

2 a 2   e 1   i 2   m 9   q 5

   b 6   f 4   j 2   n 3   r 9

   c 1   g 4   k 5   o 9   s 4

   d 4   h 4   l 2   p 24

Fractions Review Page 124

1 a 1   c 3   e 1

   b 2   d 2   f 3

2 a 3   c 8   e 5

   b 8   d 4   f 2

3 a three-fifths   c four-fifths   e three-quarters

   b two-eighths   d one-half   f seven-eighths

4 (Sample answers provided; other answers are possible for b and d. All parts must be equal in size.)

5 (Sample answers provided; other answers are possible for a, b, c, and e. All parts must be equal in size.)

6 a, d, e

7 a purple   b green   c purple   d green

8   Adult to check

9   Adult to check

10 a 6   d 4   g 4   j 2

   b 2   e 2   h 6   k 8

   c 4   f 4   i 2   l 2

7. DECIMALS

Decimals to Hundredths

Page 126 – Example(s)

Example 4: 2 wholes, 3 tenths, 7 hundredths

237

237/100 = 2.37

Page 126 – Your Turn

    a 18, 0.18   b 97, 0.97   c 152, 1.52

Page 127 – Practice

1 a   d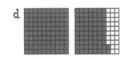

   b   e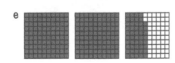

   c

2 a 1.04   b 1.99   c 0.44   d 2.43   e 2.15

3 a 91   b 72   c 36   d 41   e 50

4 a 71   d 166   g 120   j 174   m 70

   b 127   e 2   h 25   k 36

   c 46   f 89   i 152   l 101

Relating Tenths to Hundredths

Page 129 – Example(s)

Example 2: 0.70

Example 4: 0.70

Example 7: $\frac{180}{100}$ = 1.80

Page 129 – Your Turn

    a $\frac{1}{10}$, 0.10   b 60, 0.60   c 40, 0.40

Page 130 – Practice

1 a 0.70   b 1.00

2 a 1.00   b 0.30

3

	Words	Fraction	Decimal
a	five-tenths	$\frac{5}{10}$	0.50
b	six-tenths	$\frac{6}{10}$	0.60
c	ten-tenths	$\frac{10}{10}$	1.00

4 a $\frac{7}{10}$ = $\frac{70}{100}$

    7 tenths = 70 hundredths

   b $\frac{8}{10}$ = $\frac{80}{100}$

    8 tenths = 80 hundredths

   c $\frac{9}{10}$ = $\frac{90}{100}$

    9 tenths = 90 hundredths

Writing Decimals

Page 131 – Example(s)

Example 4: (both green blanks) 2

(both blue blanks) 4

(both red blanks) 9

(black blank) 249

Page 131 – Your Turn

	Fraction	Decimal	Out of 100
a	$\frac{10}{100}$	0.10	10 out of 100
b	$\frac{93}{100}$	0.93	93 out of 100
c	$\frac{312}{100}$	3.12	312 out of 100

Page 132 – Practice

1 a True   c False   e True   g True   i False

   b True   d True   f False   h True

2

	Diagram	Fraction	Decimal
a		$\frac{281}{100}$	2.81
b		$\frac{3}{100}$	0.03
c		$\frac{153}{100}$	1.53

3 a 0.73   c 2.77   e 7.1   g 0.1

   b 0.14   d 4.03   f 0.08   h 9.83

Place Value

Page 133 – Example(s)

Decimal	Hundreds	Tens	Ones	Point	Tenths	Hundredths
13.59		1	3	.	5	9
48.68		4	8	.	6	8
171.26	1	7	1	.	2	6
257.99	2	5	7	.	9	9

Page 133 – Your Turn

1 a 243.(6)2 b 120.(3)2 c 40.(8)4

2 a 341.2(6) b 203.2(1) c 83.0(4)

3 a 1(4).36 b 32(4).23 c 43(6).24

4 a 7(0).34 b 12(3).58 c 5(4)2.63

Page 134 – Practice

1

	Decimal	Tens	Ones	Point	Tenths	Hundredths
a	63.81	6	3	.	8	1
b	57.90	5	7	.	9	0
c	40.75	4	0	.	7	5
d	38.69	3	8	.	6	9
e	94.21	9	4	.	2	1
f	83.06	8	3	.	0	6

2 a 13.09 c 72.09 e 57.60 g 64.58
   b 47.36 d 83.95 f 92.72

3 a 5.03, 5.05, 5.15, 5.50, 5.85
   b 7.38, 8.30, 8.37, 8.70, 8.73
   c 6.19, 6.91, 9.16, 9.61, 19.6
   d 1.26, 2.61, 6.12, 6.21, 12.62
   e 5.57, 5.75, 7.55, 7.57, 7.75
   f 5.03, 10.35, 10.53, 13.10, 13.35
   g 0.34, 1.07, 1.34, 4.56, 7.89
   h 13.46, 14.36, 14.69, 14.96, 16.34

Decimals Review Page 135

1 a $\frac{4}{10}$, 0.40 e $\frac{32}{100}$, 0.32
   b $\frac{60}{100}$, 0.60 f $\frac{1}{10}$, 0.10
   c $\frac{2}{10}$, 0.20 g $\frac{90}{100}$, 0.90
   d $\frac{70}{100}$, 0.70 h $\frac{3}{10}$, 0.30

2 a $3\frac{72}{100} = 3.72$

   b $2\frac{99}{100}$, 2.99

3 a 76 b 19 c 95 d 87

4 a 65 c 53 e 161
   b 179 d 121 f 120

5

	Colored squares	Fraction	Decimal
a	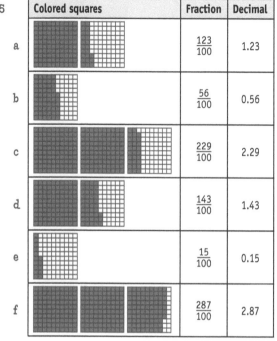	$\frac{123}{100}$	1.23
b		$\frac{56}{100}$	0.56
c		$\frac{229}{100}$	2.29
d		$\frac{143}{100}$	1.43
e		$\frac{15}{100}$	0.15
f		$\frac{287}{100}$	2.87

6 a 1.27 c 3.56 e 4.95 g 2.30
   b 0.73 d 1.09 f 0.09 h 0.17

7 a 3.(8)2 c 38.(9)5 e 493.(8)9
   b 0.(4)6 d 132.(8)6

8 a 27.4(1) c 0.9(3) e 437.2(0)
   b 137.2(5) d 1.9(2)

9 a 9(2).37 c 2(4).29 e 8(7).40
   b (0).95 d 14(7).38

10 a (1)0.36 c 1(4)3.73 e (7)1.31
    b (9)2.37 d 1(0)7.24

11 a 3.47, 3.74, 4.37, 7.34, 7.43 c 2.86, 6.28, 6.82, 8.26, 8.62
    b 1.03, 1.06, 1.24, 1.30, 1.68

8. PATTERNS

Patterns

Page 138 – Example(s)

Example 4:

Example 8: –3

Page 138 – Your Turn

1 a
   b ○□☆○□

2 a 20, 24, 28, 32, 36. Rule: + 4 b 70, 60, 50, 40, 30. Rule: – 10

Page 139 – Practice

1 a 15, 10, 5. Rule: – 5 e 70, 80, 90. Rule: + 10
   b 36, 32, 28. Rule: – 4 f 37, 47, 57. Rule: + 10
   c 54, 45, 36. Rule: – 9 g 61, 51, 41. Rule: – 10
   d 8, 10, 12. Rule: + 2

2 a

b

c D P A D P

d

e

f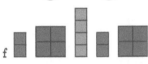

g

3	a 42, 52, 62	f 77, 73, 67	k 120, 110, 100
	b 80, 70, 40	g 70, 77, 91	l 17, 22, 37
	c 18, 21, 24	h 24, 18, 6	m 19, 24, 29
	d 19, 29, 39	i 19, 39, 59	
	e 95, 80, 70	j 8, 32, 40	

4	a Subtract	c Subtract 2	e Subtract 4
	b Add 6	d Add 3	f Subtract 5

5 a

b X O Y P <u>X</u> <u>O</u> Y P X O <u>Y</u> <u>P</u> X O <u>Y</u> P X

c

d ♥ × ○ △ ♥ × ○ △ ♥ × ○ △ ♥ × ○ △ ♥

e ⊞ ▢ ⊟ ⊠ ⊞ ▢ ⊟ ⊠ ⊞ ▢ ⊟ ⊠ ⊞ ▢ ⊟

f ⊕ ⊘ ⊗ ⊕ ⊘ ⊗ ⊕ ⊘ ⊗ ⊕ ⊘ ⊗

g B A ■ ● B <u>A</u> ■ ● B <u>A</u> ■ ● B A ■ ● B A ■

h 4 5 7 9 <u>4</u> <u>5</u> 7 9 <u>4</u> <u>5</u> <u>7</u> 9 <u>4</u> <u>5</u> <u>7</u> 9 4 5 7 <u>9</u> <u>4</u> <u>5</u> 7 9

Patterns Review Page 142

1	a ☆, **B, A**, ☆	d △, ○, ◐, △	g 18, 12, 6, 0
	b ▢, ♡, ○, ▢	e 40, 48, 56, 64	h 63, 72, 81, 90
	c △, ○, ○, △	f 60, 50, 40, 30	

2	a 15, 20, 25	d 25, 34, 52	g 126, 118, 110
	b 28, 38, 48	e 110, 90, 60	h 86, 76, 46
	c 21, 26, 36	f 75, 63, 59	

3	a Add 3	e Add 7
	b Subtract 4	f Subtract 6
	c Add 2	g Add 8
	d Subtract 5	h Subtract 10

9. LENGTH

Meters and Feet

Page 144 – Example(s)

Examples:

a 24	d 7.5	g 2
b 6	e 48	h 700
c 6	f 9,500	

Page 144 – Your Turn

Adult to check

Page 145 – Practice

1	a 1 m	c 7 m	e 1,000 cm	g 200 cm
	b 5 m	d 400 cm	f 800 cm	

2	a 5 ft.	c 12 ft.	e 48 in.	g 120 in.
	b 8 ft.	d 84 in.	f 36 in.	

3 Mark the whale, house, boat, and tree

Centimeters and Inches

Page 146 – Example(s)

Examples: Mark a, c, e, g, and i

Page 146 – Your Turn

Adult to check

Page 147 – Practice

1	a 8 cm	b 11 cm	c 5 cm	d 10 cm

2	a Adult to check	b green	c red

3 1. green 5 cm, 2. yellow 8 cm, 3. purple 9 cm, 4. orange 10 cm, 5. pink 11 cm, 6. red 14 cm

4	a 6 cm	c 9 cm	e 5 cm
	b 3 cm	d 4 cm	

5 Adult to check

6	a 2 in.	c 1 in.	e 3 in.
	b 5 in.	d 4 in.	f 4 in.

Millimeters and Quarter-Inches

Page 149 – Example(s)

Examples:

a 14	c 69	e 132
b 38	d 101	

Page 149 – Your Turn

Page 150 – Practice

1	a 83 mm	b 109 cm	c 41 mm

2	a $2\frac{3}{4}$ in.	b 5 in.	c $2\frac{1}{4}$ in.

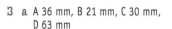

3 a A 36 mm, B 21 mm, C 30 mm,   c 33 mm
      D 63 mm
                                    d 15 mm
   b B, C, A, D

Perimeter

Page 151 – Example(s)
Examples:
   a 12 m   b 12 in.

Page 151 – Your Turn
1 a P = 4 m + 4 m + 2 m + 3 m
       = 13 m

   b P = 3 in. + 2 in. + 3 in. + 4 in.
       = 12 in.

Page 152 – Practice
1 a 10 in.   c 8 ft.   e 11 cm   g 12 in.

   b 18 mm   d 10 cm   f 12 yd.

Length Review Page 153

1 a 12, in.   b 100, m
2 Adult to check

3
	Centimeters	Meters
a	100 cm	1 m
b	300 cm	3 m
c	500 cm	5 m
d	600 cm	6 m
e	800 cm	8 m
f	200 cm	2 m

	Inches	Feet
a	24 in.	2 ft.
b	60 in.	5 ft.
c	84 in.	7 ft.
d	36 in.	3 ft.
e	48 in.	4 ft.
f	108 in.	9 ft.

4 Adult to check
5 a 14 cm   b 8 cm   c 10 cm   d 2 cm

6 a Adult to check   f 12 cm
   b blue   g 1. blue
   c purple   2. orange
   d blue, pink, orange   3. pink
   e purple   4. green
                                     5. purple

7 a $1\frac{1}{4}$ in.   c 3 in.   e $5\frac{3}{4}$ in.

   b $2\frac{1}{2}$ in.   d $4\frac{1}{2}$ in.

8 a 88 mm   c 106 mm   e 31 mm
   b 24 mm   d 3 mm

9 a P = 6 cm + 6 cm + 1 cm + 1 cm = 14 cm
   b P = 4 in. + 4 in. + 4 in. + 4 in. = 16 in.
   c P = 3 cm + 5 cm + 4 cm = 12 cm
   d P = 2 ft. + 3 ft. + 4 ft. + 3 ft. = 12 ft.
   e P = 4 m + 2 m + 4 m + 2 m = 12 m
   f P = 2 in. + 2 in. + 2 in. + 2 in. + 2 in. + 2 in. + 2 in. + 2 in.
       = 16 in.

10. ANGLES

Angles

Page 156 – Example(s)
Examples: Arms should be red, angles should be blue, and green dots should be on the vertices.

Page 156 – Your Turn
Adult to check

Page 157 – Practice
1 Adult to check
2 Adult to check
3 Adult to check

Right Angles

Page 158 – Example(s)
Examples:
   a yes   b no   c no   d yes

Page 158 – Your Turn
Adult to check

Page 159 – Practice
1 Mark a, b, c, f, i
2 Adult to check
3 Adult to check
4 a <   c =
   b =   d >

5 a   b   c

Acute and Obtuse Angles

Page 160 – Example(s)
Example 1: Adult to check
Example 2: Adult to check

Page 160 – Your Turn
   a obtuse   c acute   e acute
   b acute   d obtuse

Page 161 – Practice
1 Adult to check
2 a 3, 2, 5, 4, 1   b 4, 2, 5, 1, 3

ANSWERS

3 a obtuse   b obtuse   c acute
  d acute   e obtuse   f acute
  g acute   h obtuse   i obtuse

4 Adult to check

5 a   b   c   d

Angles Review Page 162

1 Adult to check
2 Adult to check
3 Adult to check
4 Adult to check
5 Adult to check

6 a   b   c   d

7 a acute   c obtuse   e acute
  b obtuse   d obtuse

8 a obtuse d obtuse g acute
  b acute   e obtuse h acute
  c acute   f obtuse

9 a 4, 2, 3, 1, 5
  b 2, 5, 1, 4, 3

11. SHAPES

Different Types of Lines
Page 164 – Example(s)

Page 164 – Your Turn
Adult to check

Page 165 – Practice
1 c
2 a
3 b, d
4 c, d

5 a   b   c   d

6 Adult to check

Triangles
Page 166 – Example(s)

Page 166 – Your Turn
a isosceles c equilateral e right g isosceles
b equilateral d equilateral f scalene

Page 167 – Practice
1 Adult to check
2 Right triangle: b   Scalene triangle: c, e
  Isosceles triangle: a, d   Equilateral triangle: f

Quadrilaterals
Page 168 – Example(s)
a irregular   c regular
b irregular   d irregular

Page 168 – Your Turn

Page 169 – Practice
1 square f; rhombus g; rectangle b, c; parallelogram a, e; kite d
2 Adult to check
3 regular: d, e, i
  irregular: a, b, c, f, g, h

Symmetry
Page 170 – Example(s)

a   b   c   d

Page 170 – Your Turn

a   b   c   d

 © Shell Education

ANSWERS

Page 171 – Practice

1 Symmetrical: b, c, e, f, g. Not symmetrical: a, f

2 a

   b A, B, C, E, G, H

   c D, F

   d B, G

3 Adult to check

4 a   b   c

Shapes Review Page 172

1

	Name	No. angles	No. sides	No. corners
a	equilateral triangle	3	3	3
b	square	4	4	4
c	rectangle	4	4	4
d	parallelogram	4	4	4
e	irregular quadrilateral	4	4	4

2 Adult to check

3 a right   c isosceles

   b equilateral   d scalene

4 Scalene triangle: All angles different sizes; All sides different lengths

   Isosceles triangle: Two angles the same size; Two sides the same length

   Right triangle: One right angle

   Equilateral triangle: All sides the same length; A regular shape; All angles the same size

5 a rectangle   c rhombus   e trapezoid

   b square   d parallelogram   f kite

6 square a; rhombus h; rectangle d; parallelogram b, f; trapezoid g; kite c

7 Circle: a, b, e, f

8 Adult to check

9 b   e

10 Adult to check

11 a   b

   c   d

12. AREA

Area

Page 176 – Example(s)

a   b   c

Page 176 – Your Turn

Adult to check

Page 177 – Practice

1 a   b
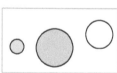

2 a second shape   c third shape   e second shape

   b second shape   d first shape

3 a second shape   b third shape

4 a 1, 3, 2, 4, 5   b 1, 3, 4, 2, 5   c 3, 2, 1, 4, 5

Measuring Area with Units

Page 178 – Example(s)

a 30   b 16   c 32

Page 178 – Your Turn

a 12

b 6

Page 179 – Practice

1 a 103   b 87

2 a 12   d green   g 20

   b 24   e 8   h 68

   c purple   f 12

Measuring Areas Using a Grid

Page 180 – Example(s)
a 11   b 12

Page 180 – Your Turn
a 35

b 16

Page 181 – Practice
1 a 16   b 4   c 20

2 Adult to check

3 Tall Tales: 10; China Today: 16; Tiny Tales: 6

4 a 4   b 4   c 10   d 14

Square Centimeters and Inches

Page 182 – Example(s)
a length, width
1 cm, 4 cm
4

b length, width
2 in., 3 in.
6

Page 182 – Your Turn
a length × width
= 2 cm × 5 cm
= 10 cm²

Page 183 – Practice
1 a seven square centimeters, 7 cm²

b eight square centimeters, 8 cm²

c ten square centimeters, 10 cm²

d sixteen square centimeters, 16 cm²

2 a E   b A   c D

3 Adult to check

Square Meters and Feet

Page 184 – Example(s)
a length, width
2 ft., 4 ft.
8

b length, width
3 m, 3 m
9

Page 184 – Your Turn
pencil case, book

Page 185 – Practice
1 Adult to check

2 a 27 m²   b 2 m²   c 8 m²

3 a shed   b pool   c 70 m²   d 2 m²

4 Adult to check

5 Adult to check

Shapes with the Same Area

Page 186 – Example(s)
a A = 10 in.²

b Adult to check. Shapes should be composed of 10 squares.

c Adult to check. Shapes should be composed of 10 squares.

Page 186 – Your Turn
Adult to check

Page 187 – Practice
1 Adult to check

2 a A, E, F, G   c 12 in.²

b B, C, D, H   d 8 in.²

Perimeter

Page 188 – Example(s)
a 12   b 12

Page 188 – Your Turn
a 2 cm + 5 cm + 2 cm + 5 cm
= 14 cm

b 2 in. + 1 in. + 1 in. + 2 in. + 3 in. + 3 in.
= 12 in.

Page 189 – Practice
1 a B = 2 cm + 1 cm + 1 cm + 1 cm + 1 cm + 1 cm + 2 cm + 3 cm
= 12 cm

b C = 3 cm + 1 cm + 1 cm + 1 cm + 1 cm + 1 cm + 3 cm + 1 cm +
1 cm + 1 cm + 1 cm + 1 cm = 16 cm

c D = 2 cm + 2 cm + 1 cm + 2 cm + 1 cm + 4 cm
= 12 cm

d E = 4 cm + 5 cm + 1 cm + 1 cm + 1 cm + 1 cm + 1 cm + 1 cm +
1 cm + 2 cm + 2 cm + 1 cm + 2 cm + 1 cm = 24 cm

e F = 1 cm + 1 cm + 1 cm + 1 cm + 1 cm + 1 cm + 1 cm + 1 cm +
1 cm + 1 cm + 1 cm + 1 cm + 2 cm + 1 cm + 1 cm + 1 cm +
1 cm + 1 cm + 1 cm + 1 cm + 2 cm = 24 cm

2 a A, B, D

b E, F

3 Adult to check

Area Review Page 190

1 a Left shape   b Right shape   c Left shape

2 Adult to check

3 a   b   c

4 a 4, 2, 3, 5, 1   b 1, 3, 4, 2, 5   c 2, 4, 5, 3, 1

5 a 12   b 24   c 60

6 a 57   b 62   c 64

7 a 16   b 14   c 13

8 a length × width
= 3 cm × 3 cm
= 9 cm²

c length × width
= 5 cm × 5 cm
= 25 cm²

b length × width
= 2 cm × 2 cm
= 4 cm²

9 a length × width
= 3 in. × 5 in.
= 15 in.²

c length × width
= 2 in. × 4 in.
= 8 in.²

b length × width
= 1 in. × 5 in.
= 5 in.²

10 a 5 cm²   c 7 cm²   e 17 cm²
b 10 cm²   d 14 cm²

11 Adult to check
12 a Adult to check
b Adult to check

13 a 5 m²   c 12 m²   e 7 m²
b 25 m²   d 15 m²   f 9 m²

14 a 6 m²   c 15 m²   e 2 m²
b 28 m²   d 6 m²   f 96 m²

15 a House   b Shed

16 a 13 m²   b 4 m²   c 9 m²   d 26 m²

17 Color: 1, 4, 5, 6, 7, 9

18 a 14 ft.   b 14 cm   c 23 m   d 18 in.

13. CAPACITY

Capacity

Page 196 – Example(s)

a   b   c

Page 196 – Your Turn

Adult to check

Page 197 – Practice

1 a 3, 1, 2, 5, 4
b 5, 3, 1, 2, 4

2 a 1
b medicine cup: 20; glass: 10; mug: 7
c medicine cup
d pot

Liters and Gallons

Page 198 – Example(s)

a 1 gal.   c 5 gal.
b 3 L   d 2 L

Page 198 – Your Turn

sink, bathtub, pool

Page 199 – Practice

1 Circle a, c, e, f, i

2 Adult to check

3 Color: Cola 10 bottles; Lemonade 7 bottles; Orange soda 3 bottles.

Measuring Liters and Gallons

Page 200 – Example(s)

a   b   c   d

Page 200 – Your Turn

a 3 L   c 1 gal.   e 2 L
b 1 gal.   d 4 L   f 5 gal.

Page 201 – Practice

1 a Color 4 bottles   c Color 5 bottles
b Color 10 bottles

2 b   c   d

3 a C
b A or D
c Pitcher B: 3 gal., Pitcher C: 4 gal., Pitcher D: 6 gal.

Milliliters, Cups, and Fluid Ounces

Page 202 – Example(s)

Examples: Mark a, b, e, and f.

ANSWERS

Page 202 – Your Turn

2 a b

c d

e

Page 203 – Practice

1 a $\frac{1}{4}$ L b $\frac{3}{4}$ L c $\frac{1}{2}$ L

2 a 3,000 mL b 1,500 mL c 2,250 mL

3 a $\frac{3}{4}$ c. b $\frac{1}{4}$ c. c $\frac{1}{2}$ c.

4 a 16 fl. oz. b 20 fl. oz. c 14 fl. oz.

Capacity Review Page 204

1 Adult to check

2 a tea cup 80; glass 20; beach bucket 8; pot 4; fish bowl 2

 b tea cup

 c fish bowl

3 1, 3, 2, 5, 4

4 Adult to check

5 Adult to check

6 a 3 b 7 c 1

7 a b

c d

8 a 500 mL b 1,000 mL c 250 mL d 750 mL

9 a 6 fl. oz. b 8 fl. oz. c 2 fl. oz. d 4 fl. oz.

10 a b

c d

e f

11 a $\frac{1}{4}$ L b 1 L c $\frac{1}{2}$ L d $\frac{1}{4}$ L

12 a 1,500 mL b 2,250 mL c 3,500 mL d 1,750 mL

13 a 1 c. b $\frac{1}{4}$ c. c $\frac{3}{4}$ c. d $\frac{1}{2}$ c.

14 a 20 fl. oz. b 14 fl. oz. c 10 fl. oz. d 28 fl. oz.

14. MASS

Kilograms and Pounds

Page 208 – Example(s)

Examples: Circle a, e, f, and i.

Page 208 – Your Turn

Adult to check

Page 209 – Practice

1 a 83 pounds — 10 lbs.×8, 5 lbs.×5, 1 lb.×5
 b 16 kilograms — 10 kg×10, 5 kg×5, 1 kg×5
 c 51 pounds — 10 lbs.×5, 5 lbs.×5, 1 lb.×5

2 a 32 b 97 c 19

3 a 23 kg b 10 lbs. c 17 kg d 1 lbs. e 94 kg

4 a ✗ c ✗ e ✗ g ✗
 b ✔ d ✔ f ✗

5 a 8 b 16 c 1 d 2

6 Tick: a, c, d, g, h, i, j

7 a coconuts e 5 kg
 b pineapple f pineapple, cantaloupe, oranges, watermelon, coconut
 c 4
 d watermelon and coconuts

8 a 18 lbs. b 45 lbs. c 18 lbs. d 6 lbs.

9 a a chicken c a boy e a carton of milk
 b a watermelon d 2 L milk

ANSWERS

10 Adult to check

11 a E

b C

c A and B: 17 kg; C and D: 35 kg; E and D: 13 kg

d 145 kg

Grams and Ounces

Page 212 – Example(s)

Examples: Circle the tennis ball, candy, party hat, pen, and popcorn.

Page 212 – Your Turn

Adult to check

Page 213 – Practice

1 a 9 oz   c 102 g   e 98 g

b 14 g oz   d 80 oz   f 6,115 g

2 a 3   c 2   e 5   g 1

b 7   d 6   f 8

3 a chickpeas

b spice

c peas, beans, tuna, corn, soup, spice

d tomatoes, chickpeas

4 pencil, egg, feather, lime

Mass Review Page 214

1 a kilograms, pounds   b kg, lb.

2 Circle b, c, e, f, g

3 Color:

a 3 × 10 lbs., 2 × 1 lbs.

b 1 × 10 kg, 1 × 5 kg, 3 × 1 kg

c 4 × 10 lbs., 1 × 1 lbs.

d 5 × 10 kg, 2 × 1 kg

4 a 83 kg   b 29 lbs.   c 114 kg

5 a 6 kg   c 50 kg   e 193 kg   g 99 kg

b 29 lbs.   d 84 lbs.   f 205 lbs.   h 78 lbs.

6 a ✔   c ✗   e ✗   g ✔

b ✗   d ✔   f ✗   h ✔

7 a D   d 24 lbs.   g 72 lbs.

b C   e 8 lbs.   h C, A, E, B, D

c B and C   f 36 lbs.

8 a carton of milk   d a package of meat

b a small dog   e an adult

c a baby   f a pineapple

9 Adult to check

10 Circle a, b, d, g, h

11 a 702 g   d 15 oz.   g 80 g   j 720 oz.

b 99 oz.   e 373 g   h 106 oz.   k 3006 g

c 2620 g   f 8 oz.   i 6304 g

12 a 90 g, 100 g, 425 g, 510 g, 914 g

b tomatoes, salmon

c tomatoes, soup

d lentils, salmon, peas

e 814 g; 335 g; 420 g; 489 g

f 575 g; 910 g; 86 g; 490 g; 900 g

15. TIME

Timetables

Page 219 – Example(s)

a 5   c 7:33

b 4   d Lotus Lane

Page 219 – Your Turn

a Cherry Lane   b 12   c 4

Page 220 – Practice

1 a red   h 65 minutes

b red group   i 90 minutes

c green   j 75 minutes

d 9:00   k 4

e 3:15   l 2 hours 15 minutes

f 11:15   m 6 hours 15 minutes

g 1:45

2 a 15 minutes   d 50 minutes   g 11:30 am

b 45 minutes   e 25 minutes   h 2:35 pm

c 30 minutes   f 1 hour   i 3:15 pm

3 a 8:57   b 9:40   c Good morning

4 a 9:33   b 9:27   c 10:08

5 a 58 mins   b 27 mins   c 29 mins

Time Review Page 223

1 a Room 12   c Room 10   e 30 minutes   g 5½ hours

b Room 14   d 4   f 12:30 pm

2 a 4:45   d 12 minutes; 9 minutes; 21 minutes; 52 minutes

b 4:33

c 4:32

3 a 6 stops   b 2 stops   c 5 stops

NOTES

© Shell Education